RIGHTS GU
FOR HOME O\

revised by

Simon Ennals
Sue Spaull
and
Lorraine Thompson

7th Edition
1988

SHAC
(The London Housing Aid Centre)
189a Old Brompton Road, London SW5
Tel: 01-373 7841/7276

CPAG Ltd
Child Poverty Action Group
1-5 Bath Street, London EC1
Tel: 01-253 3406

CPAG Ltd ISBN 0 946744 12 2

SHAC ISBN 0 948857 24 2

Typeset by Boldface Typesetters, 17a Clerkenwell Road, London EC1

Printed by RAP Ltd, 201 Spotland Road, Rochdale OL12 7AF

CPAG

The Child Poverty Action Group is a national charity primarily concerned with the position of families on low incomes and those dependent upon welfare benefits. CPAG publishes a wide range of materials on these issues and its Citizens' Rights Office produces two annual guides to the systems of means-tested and other benefits (respectively the *National Welfare Benefits Handbook* and the *Rights Guide to Non-Means-Tested Social Security Benefits*). The Citizens' Rights Office has considerable experience of the difficulties facing those on benefits through its service of advice and information to local advice agencies.

Simon Ennals is a freelance trainer and consultant on welfare rights issues. He has worked in CPAG's Citizens' Rights Office, and in local authority welfare rights offices.

SHAC

SHAC opened in 1969 as London's first independent housing aid centre. Its work covers the whole range of housing problems, including homelessness, security of tenure, disrepair and mortgage arrears. Over the past 19 years, SHAC has given advice and help to over 115,000 households.

SHAC's publications and training courses draw on this direct advice-giving experience; it produces a range of advice booklets, published research into major housing issues and provides information and training for a wide range of voluntary and statutory organisations.

For further information about SHAC publications, contact the Information Office; for details of training courses, contact the Courses and Conferences Organiser (both at SHAC, 189c Brompton Rd, London SW5).

Sue Spaull has worked as a housing adviser in both statutory and voluntary sectors. She is currently a caseworker and trainer at SHAC.

Lorraine Thompson is a principal member of SHAC's casework team. She specialises in mortgage debt advice.

ACKNOWLEDGEMENTS

This edition of the *Rights Guide for Home Owners* builds upon the valuable work of others who prepared the original text and its subsequent revisions. The authors particularly thank: Ken Baublys, Lorna Findlay, Beth Lakhani, Jan Luba, Jim Read, Jo Tunnard, Clare Whately, Sue Witherspoon and John Gallagher.

Thanks are also due to Carol Brickley and June Taylor at Boldface who designed and typeset the Guide; to Julia Lewis (CPAG) who saw it through production; and to Christine Jamieson (SHAC) and Peter Ridpath (CPAG) who promoted the finished work.

Contents

Introduction

Under present government policies, more and more people are being encouraged to buy their own homes. Home ownership, once the privilege of the better off, is now the most common form of tenure.

Yet the rise in home ownership is currently taking place against a background of massive unemployment. A mortgage which a person has managed quite happily whilst in work can become a serious burden when that person is faced with the sudden drop in income brought about by unemployment. Building societies have experienced a dramatic rise in arrears largely on account of this. Between 1979 and 1984, the figures for unemployment nationally trebled. During the period from the end of 1979 to June 1986 building society arrears rose nearly eightfold and the number of properties taken into possession rose almost sevenfold.

All too often a small amount of mortgage arrears, brought about by a drop in income, or an unexpected event like marriage break-up, has been the start of a cycle which has led to a family becoming homeless. *Yet this need not happen.*

There are many steps which a family can take to maintain their mortgage repayments and thus keep their home. Borrowers and their advisers must consider the mortgage arrangements, the best use of welfare benefits and tax allowances, and aspects of property and family law, as well as the availability of alternative accommodation. Sadly, in our experience, lenders, solicitors and other advisers have not always had the necessary knowledge to advise families on the best way to keep their homes.

This Guide explains what can be done. We give practical, step-by-step advice on how to cut mortgage costs, increase income and negotiate with lenders, the courts, social security offices and local authorities. Because mortgage difficulties often arise when a relationship breaks down, we have given special attention to the problems faced by the single parent who is left with the children and threatened with loss of the home.

Much of this Guide draws attention to the help home owners can receive from the social security system. Recent legislation has meant that the structure of welfare benefits changed dramatically in April 1988. These changes have been incorporated into the welfare benefits chapters in the Guide (Chapters 3 and 4), and are referred to in other chapters where relevant.

We also include a section on repairs and improvements and suggest ways of meeting the cost of such work.

All the suggestions we make have been tried and tested by borrowers we have advised. We hope that, by using this Guide, many more people will be able to keep their homes, secure from the threat of financial hardship and homelessness.

The law and procedures are described as we understand them to be on 1 August 1988.

Simon Ennals
Sue Spaull
Lorraine Thompson

CHAPTER ONE

Different kinds of mortgages

This part of the Guide explains the different kinds of mortgage available, how they work and who you may be able to get your loan from. It goes on to cover the ways in which the government helps you pay your mortgage.

If you are facing high mortgage payments and want to cut the cost you must first sort out exactly:

- ☐ how many mortgages you have (you could well have more than one);
- ☐ what kind of mortgages they are (ie, what arrangements you have made for repaying each one);
- ☐ what help you are receiving from the government (see page 10).

This section will be particularly useful if you have not had much to do with your mortgage(s) until now; for instance, if you have been left on your own in the home by your partner. However, if you do understand your mortgage(s), you could move on to the next chapter to see how to cut your costs, and simply refer back when necessary.

MORTGAGE VOCABULARY

A **mortgage** is a type of loan which gives the lender the right to recover their money by taking over your home and selling it if you fail to make the agreed repayments.

Your **repayments** are the instalments you pay to your lender every month. There will be two parts to each repayment:

- ☐ **Interest**: this is the price you have to pay for borrowing the money; and

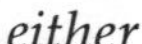

either

- **Capital**: this is the word used for the money you have borrowed and are paying back directly to your lender;
  or
- **Endowment premium**: this is the phrase used for the monthly payment which you make to a life assurance company. Instead of paying directly to your lender, you save with the company. The company agrees to pay back the full amount you have borrowed to your lender at the end of an agreed period (or on your death if you die before the end of that period).

The **term** is the word used for the number of years over which you have borrowed money and have agreed to pay it back.

The rights that a mortgage lender has against the borrower are secured by registering a **charge**, either at the appropriate District Land Registry or, if the land is unregistered, at the Land Charges Registry in Plymouth. The existence of a charge has two important consequences:

- The lenders can apply to a court for an order to sell your home to get their money back if you do not make the agreed repayments (or are in some other breach of the mortgage agreement); *and*
- You must repay your lenders the sum outstanding on your mortgage when you sell your home. (Before a property can change hands the charges must be removed; when the charge is a mortgage, it will only be removed when the loan is repaid.)

Every mortgage you have will be registered as a charge. These will be listed in the order in which you borrowed the money so that the first lender will have the 'first charge', the second lender will have the 'second charge', and so on. This is the order in which the lenders will be repaid if your home is sold.

The **equity** is the difference between the sale value of your home, and the value of the mortgage 'charged' against it.

Example:
Suppose you sell your home for £50,000 and you have two mortgages. £25,000 is still owing to the building society who lent you the money to buy it in the first place, and £6,000 is still owing to the finance company who lent you the money to put in central heating and buy a car.

Sale value of home	£50,000
The building society has the 'first charge' and takes the first	£25,000
The finance company has the 'second charge' and takes the next	£6,000
The remainder is your 'equity'	£19,000

TYPES OF MORTGAGE

You may have more than one mortgage and each may be a different type of mortgage. Check all your loans carefully to make sure you know exactly what you have.

There are three main types of mortgage:

- ☐ **Capital repayment (or annuity) mortgages** where you repay the capital gradually over the term, in your monthly instalments;
- ☐ **Endowment mortgages** where you pay interest only to the lender, and pay an 'endowment premium' to a life assurance company;
- ☐ **Bridging loans** where you take on a temporary loan so that you can buy your home while you are waiting for your money to come from your long-term lender.

HOW MORTGAGES WORK

When you borrow money, you obviously have to repay it. But the method of repayment varies with the type of mortgage. These are described below:

Capital repayment (or annuity) mortgages

If you have a capital repayment mortgage, your monthly instalments are made up of the interest you pay on the amount borrowed and repayment of the loan itself (called **capital**). Unless the interest rate changes, your monthly repayments remain the same throughout the period of your mortgage.

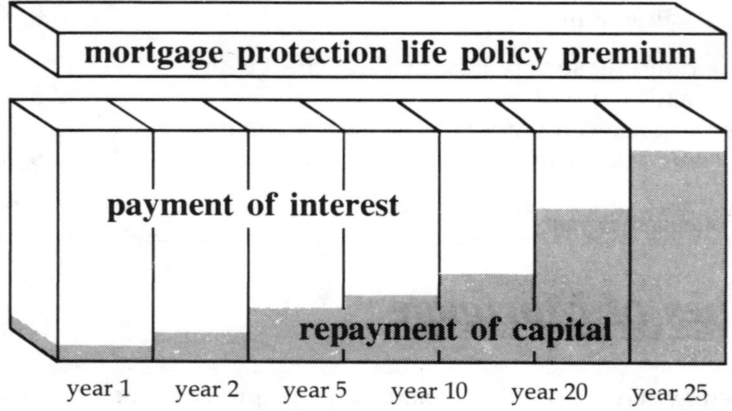

In the first year of your mortgage, most of your monthly repayment is interest on the loan and only a tiny amount is paying off the capital. Your monthly mortgage payments in the second year will be the same, but will consist of slightly less interest than in the first year and a little more capital will be paid off. As each year goes by, you will pay off more of the amount borrowed. As you pay interest on a smaller and smaller amount, more capital is paid off and, by the end of the loan period, your payment is almost all capital with only a tiny amount of interest.

The top part of the above diagram shows a very important third part of your monthly payments. This is the small payment that makes sure that your family are not left with the worry of repaying the loan if you die before the end of the term. The payment is for a **mortgage protection policy**. Your building society will offer to arrange mortgage protection cover when you take out a capital repayment mortgage, or you may arrange your own cover.

Endowment mortgages

Endowment mortgages are different from capital repayment mortgages because the capital is not repaid gradually year by year but is paid back all at once at the end of the mortgage term. To make sure that you will be able to pay it back at the end, you take out an endowment policy with a life assurance company. In return for your monthly payment of insurance premiums, the life assurance company agrees to pay the lender a lump sum at the end of your loan (or on your death if earlier).

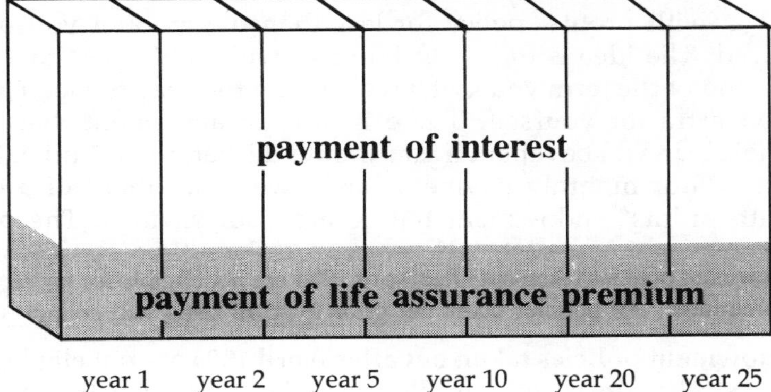

You pay interest on the loan and your insurance premium each month but, because you do not repay any of the money until the end of the term, the interest will remain the same each year. Your repayments will only change if the interest rate rises or falls.

There are three different kinds of endowment life policy which can be used to repay a mortgage. Look at your own policy to find out which you have.

- ☐ A **'guaranteed'** or **'non-profit' endowment**. This is where the life assurance company agrees to pay the amount of money you borrowed at the end of the term (or on your death, if you die before then) and does no more than that. This policy probably offers the worst value for money. Many second mortgages are covered by this kind of endowment policy.

- ☐ A **'with profits' endowment**. This is where the life assurance company agrees to do two things. First, it will repay at the end of the term the money you borrowed. Second, it will give you some extra money which it calls 'profits', 'bonuses' or 'dividends'. You will have to pay higher premiums to get this extra sum. The company decides every few years what the bonuses should be and they are stored up for you. If you should die before the end of the mortgage term, the whole loan will be repaid.

  This kind of policy offers a built-in savings scheme but has the highest monthly premiums. A *Which* report in May 1986 concluded that if you want to save, you would do better to invest in a separate savings scheme rather than link it to your mortgage.

- ☐ A **'low cost'** or **'build up' endowment**. This is where you take out a 'with profits' policy for less than the amount you borrowed. The idea is that your bonuses will build up so that by the end of the term you will have enough to repay the loan and a bit extra for yourself. There is also an agreement that the whole loan will be repaid if you should die before the end of the term. Your monthly payments are lower than those of a full 'with profits' endowment but so are your savings. The premiums for a low-cost endowment are less than those for a guaranteed or non-profit policy.

Endowment policies taken out after April 1984 are not eligible for tax relief on premiums. Policies taken out prior to April 1984 will continue to receive 15 per cent tax relief on policy premiums if the terms of the policy are not changed, up until 6 April 1989 when tax relief will be cut to 12.5 per cent.

Which is best?

Normally capital repayment mortgages are best for most people because:

- ☐ They are cheaper. Usually, endowment mortgages are charged at a higher rate of interest. In addition, tax relief on premiums which you would pay under an endowment mortgage is no longer available;
- ☐ Although the monthly outgoings on a low-cost endowment mortgage can be comparable to the cost of a capital repayment mortgage, capital repayment mortgages are much more flexible if you have financial difficulties and need to re-arrange your finances.

Bridging loans

Unlike the two types of mortgages described above, there is no arrangement for repaying a bridging loan built in to your loan agreement. A bridging loan is only granted to 'bridge' a gap until money comes through from another source (this might be cash from the sale of another home, or it might be the advance of your mortgage money). You have to repay the loan as soon as the money is available, and you have to pay interest on the loan until then. The interest you have to pay will be higher than building society and local authority interest rates. Never take out a bridging loan unless you are absolutely certain that the amount of money you need will be forthcoming at a particular date. A bridging loan will not usually be granted for more than a year. When the agreed time is up you may be put under pressure to sell your home in order to repay (but see Chapter Six).

TYPES OF LENDERS

Lenders of money guaranteed by a mortgage are called **mortgagees**, and borrowers are called **mortgagors**. To make it easier reading, this Guide talks about 'lenders' and 'borrowers'.

There are several kinds of lenders. They can vary greatly as to the kind of mortgage they will offer, the rates of interest they will charge, and the maximum number of years over which the loan can be paid back.

Building societies

First mortgages are usually with building societies, because they are the largest lenders. Building societies normally grant mortgages which are used either to buy or to improve a home and then only if they can register the first charge. They can lend for repairs (see page 23). Building society mortgages are among the cheapest available and they allow long repayment terms (sometimes up to 35 years). They grant mortgages on both the **capital repayment** and **endowment** methods (see pages 12-15). All major building societies belong to the Building Societies' Association which recommends the interest rate to charge, and the general code of practice (see Appendix 10). However, individual societies are free to set their own interest rates. Societies may have different lending policies and often the local branch managers have some discretion in deciding what to do in individual cases. Building societies' power to lend money is set out in Section 10 of the Building Societies Act 1986.

Local authorities

Local authorities have power to lend money to enable people to buy, improve or repair their homes. Normally they will only lend if they can register the first charge (see page 2), but they do have the power to take the second charge on loans for improvement or repair. They generally lend on older properties and may charge higher rates of interest than building societies. They only lend on a capital repayment basis. Local authorities should be particularly helpful where one of their borrowers has difficulty in making repayments, as they may have to rehouse someone evicted for non-payment (see page 102).

However, because of financial cutbacks in recent years, most local authorities will now only lend to council tenants wishing to buy their homes. Where such a tenant wishes to buy his or her home under the Right to Buy provisions of the Housing Act 1985, Part V, the local authority is required to provide a loan if the tenant wants one. The authority may provide the loan themselves or arrange a loan through a building society. However, tenants are free to arrange a mortgage with another lender if they prefer to do so.

Insurance companies

Granting mortgages is not the main business of insurance companies. Many of them will not grant first mortgages at all, or will consider them only for more expensive properties. They lend only on an endowment basis. The most common way in which insurance companies are involved in the granting of mortgages is by providing endowment life assurance policies to people borrowing on that basis from building societies. Insurance companies also sometimes lend **'topping-up' mortgages** and take a second charge where a building society has the first charge. This usually happens when the building society has refused to lend as much as the borrower needs. Only take out a second mortgage if you are absolutely sure that the first lender will not lend you more. It is important to work out how much the second mortgage will cost and whether you can afford the extra repayments. If you must have a second mortgage, you will usually get a much cheaper one from an insurance company than from a finance company.

Banks

Banks lend in two ways:

- **First mortgages for buying or improving a home** are normally over a 20 or 25-year period at interest rates similar to those of the building societies.
- **Second loans for any purpose**, for example installing central heating or buying a car, are likely to be over a shorter period such as 10 years. They are relatively expensive because the monthly payments need to be high to repay the loan in such a short time, and are likely to be at a higher interest rate than a first loan.

Banks can grant either capital repayment or endowment mortgages.

Finance companies

You may have bought your home with a finance company mortgage, or you may have borrowed from them later with a second mortgage, to pay for central heating, a car, furniture, etc. Your repayments are probably very high, both because finance companies charge up to 35 per cent rate of interest (although you may have to look carefully at the small print to find the true rate), and because they will only lend over a fairly short term, at most about 15 years. Smaller finance companies and credit brokers have been known to charge as much as 68 per cent rate of interest. You may also find that you were charged a fee for the mortgage when you took it out (which could be one-tenth of your loan), and that you are also paying interest on this fee (called a **'guarantee'** or **'indemnity' premium**).

A finance company mortgage could land you in serious trouble, both because the monthly costs are often higher than you think at the beginning, and also because once you start missing payments arrears build up very quickly. If you try to pay back (or **'redeem'**) the whole loan, you may find that you owe far more than you originally borrowed. It is now possible to ask the courts to change the terms of a loan agreement, even if it has been arranged a long time ago, under Sections 137 to 140 of the Consumer Credit Act 1974. These sections give the court the power to set aside the whole or any part of the obligation imposed on the borrower and can require the lender to repay all or some of the payments made. If you wish to challenge the terms of your agreement you will need good advice from a solicitor (see Appendix 7).

GOVERNMENT HELP WITH YOUR MORTGAGE

The government provides assistance for those paying off a mortgage if the money is used to buy or improve the home. The help takes the form of giving full tax relief on the interest payments that are made and is available for the first £30,000 of the loan.

Under the **MIRAS (Mortgage Interest Relief At Source**) system, introduced in April 1983, most borrowers with loans of up to £30,000 pay mortgage interest to their lender with the basic rate of tax (25 per cent from 1 April 1988) already deducted. No adjustments to their tax allowances will be necessary for borrowers paying basic rate tax. (Borrowers paying very little or no income tax also come within MIRAS.) For those paying higher rate tax, there will be an entitlement to additional tax relief.

Until April 1987, loans above £30,000 may or may not have come within MIRAS; this was up to the lender. If the loan was not within MIRAS, all of the tax relief due would be claimed from the Inland Revenue as a tax allowance. However, from April 1987 new and existing loans of above £30,000 were also included in the MIRAS system. Tax relief at the basic rate is deducted by the lender on interest up to £30,000. Interest payments net of tax relief are made direct to the lender.

From 1 August 1988, tax relief will be limited to £30,000 per property. After this date unmarried mortgage sharers will only receive tax relief on the first £30,000 of the loan instead of up to £30,000 each. Existing mortgage sharers and those who have a formal offer of a loan *and* who have signed a contract by 1 August 1988 will continue to receive tax relief on up to £30,000 each.

CHAPTER TWO

Cutting your mortgage costs

If you are not able to make the monthly payments to your lenders you risk losing your home. Any of the lenders can apply to the court for an order to sell your home, and may be given this unless you can show that you can and will manage in future.

If you are in difficulties with your payments, discuss these first with your lender. Your lender can help by looking at ways of rearranging your payments either temporarily or permanently to help you manage. *Do not stop paying*. It is better to pay what you can while, at the same time, looking at ways of cutting your costs.

This chapter explains how you can reduce your monthly mortgage costs by rearranging your loan(s) and also describes the best way to approach your lenders with your proposals. The following arrangements have all been reached by people having difficulties with their mortgages. However, you might well be told that your own proposals are not acceptable. Do not let this put you off. Most lenders, but especially building societies and local authorities, have such wide powers that they can accept almost any proposal they consider appropriate. Remember that it would cause your lender time and trouble to evict you. They will usually prefer to let you keep the loan going if you can show that you can manage. A lot will depend on how you set out your suggestions for paying in the future. If you are under pressure from your lenders because you have arrears, see Chapter Six for how you can try to clear these. However, if you want to show your lender that your arrears can be cleared, you must at the same time convince them (and yourself) that you will be able to keep up your payments in the future. This chapter will help you do this. Even if you cannot come to any agreement and you are taken to court to be evicted, do not give up hope. Tell the court what you have suggested. The court may agree that your proposals are reasonable and give you time to show that you can manage.

IF YOU HAVE ONE MORTGAGE

Capital repayment mortgage

There are two ways in which your repayment arrangement can be changed to cut your costs.

Pay mortgage interest only

Your lender may agree to accept payments of interest alone and allow you to put off paying back the capital you owe while your present difficulties last. The amount of difference this will make to your weekly payments will depend on the length of time you have had your mortgage. As shown in the diagram on page 4, the repayment of capital forms only a small part of your monthly payments in the first few years but the amount grows later on. This rearrangement need only be temporary and should not involve much work for your lender. It is worth asking them to agree to help you in this way even if it makes only a small difference to your weekly costs. You should certainly do so if you are receiving income support, as your benefit will only cover the interest part of your mortgage payments.

Ask for this whether your drop in income is temporary or permanent as it is the only way to get an immediate reduction in your costs.

Extend the term of the mortgage

You can ask your lender to extend the mortgage term in practice asking them to make a new mortgage arrangement which will give you more time to repay the money you still owe. This will reduce the capital part of your monthly payments. The amount of interest you have to pay each week will, however, remain the same.

Because this arrangement is only going to affect the capital part of your repayments, there is no point in suggesting this to your lender if they will agree to accept interest only.

If your lender will accept interest only now, you could ask for an extension of the term till the time when you can afford to start repaying the capital again. If your lender has refused to accept interest only payments you should ask to extend the term whether your drop in income is temporary or permanent.

How to negotiate with your lender

Write to your lender stating:

- ☐ your name, address and mortgage account number;
- ☐ your present financial difficulties, why they have arisen and how long they are going to last;
- ☐ that you wish to pay interest only *or* to extend the mortgage term;
- ☐ what your income is going to be in future and how you are going to keep up the new payments.

Remember to keep a copy of your letter.

> **Special note for separated partners:** You should check page 92 to see what other points you should include in your letter.

Endowment mortgage

There are two ways in which your repayment arrangements can be changed to cut your costs.

(i) Change to a capital repayment mortgage

This means that you stop paying the endowment policy premiums and instead start repaying capital. Interest payments on the money you owe will, of course, continue. Depending on the type of endowment mortgage you have, the cost of paying interest plus repayment of capital may be less than the cost of paying interest plus your policy premium.

It is possible to obtain a temporary suspension of policy premiums if you have an endowment mortgage. However, if difficulties are likely to last it may be better to change to a capital repayment mortgage even if the difference in the cost is small because it is easier to re-arrange the costs of a capital repayment mortgage.

First, you need to get information from your insurance company.

Write to the insurance company stating:

- ☐ your name, address and insurance policy number (if you know it);

- ☐ that you want to know the **surrender value** of your policy. (This is the amount the company will pay you in cash if you stop paying the premiums and cancel the policy);
- ☐ that you want to know the **paid-up value** of your policy. (This is the amount of money which the company will still agree to pay out at the end of the term or on your death if you stop paying premiums but do not cancel the policy);
- ☐ that you need this information because you are hoping to change the terms of your mortgage.

Remember to keep a copy of your letter.

Second, you need to negotiate with your building society. Your insurance policy is your lender's guarantee that their capital will be repaid and it is part of your mortgage agreement that you will pay the premiums, so you will have to discuss with them the terms on which you can make the change.

If your mortgage is directly with an insurance company, or your building society is not willing to change the terms of the mortgage, you may be able to get a new mortgage for the whole amount and pay off your existing lender (see page 15).

Special note for separated partners: If you are not named on the life policy you may not be able to get any surrender or paid-up value unless your partner cooperates. However, this will not necessarily prevent your lender from changing the endowment mortgage to a capital repayment mortgage and you should certainly ask them to if this would help.

Write to your lender stating:

- ☐ your name, address and mortgage account number;
- ☐ your present financial difficulties, why they have arisen, and how long they are likely to last;
- ☐ the insurance company's figures for the surrender value and the paid-up value of your policy;
- ☐ *either:*
  that you wish to cancel your policy and keep the surrender value to use for some necessary expense, eg, house maintenance or paying another bill (ask for this if you need cash now);

or:

that you wish to stop paying your policy premiums but not to cancel your policy. You would like that part of your mortgage which would be covered by the paid-up value to continue on the endowment basis, and only the remainder to be transferred to the capital repayment basis. If you do not need cash now, this might be a better choice as your outgoings would be lower. This is because you will be paying interest only and will not have to make capital repayments on that part of the mortgage which will be covered by the paid-up value;

- ☐ what your income is going to be in future and how you are going to keep up the new payments;
- ☐ that you wish to know what legal expenses, if any, you will be charged when the mortgage is changed.

Make sure you keep a copy of your letter.

Remember: if you do convert to a capital repayment mortgage, then you should take out a mortgage protection policy to cover the risk of your dying before the end of the term (see page 4).

(ii) Pay interest only

A change to a capital repayment mortgage will take some time to come into effect. In the meantime, your lender may agree to let you stop paying your policy premiums which will mean an immediate cut in your costs. If you are receiving income support this will be an important change, because your benefit will only cover the interest payments.

However, many insurance policies are automatically cancelled if a certain number of premiums are not paid (eg, for 6 months or more), so your lender may only agree to this kind of arrangement in the *very* short term.

IF YOU HAVE TWO OR MORE MORTGAGES

Making a fresh start

You will need to arrange all your borrowing on the cheapest possible basis; this will probably mean a new capital repayment mortgage over a long term. Sometimes this is called re-mortgaging. You should do this if:

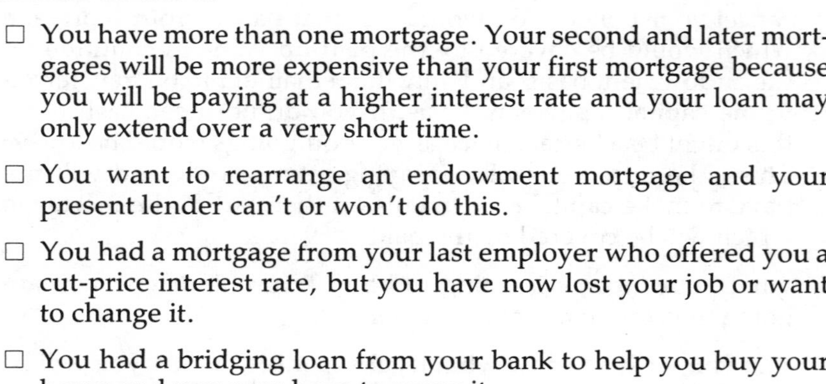

- ☐ You have more than one mortgage. Your second and later mortgages will be more expensive than your first mortgage because you will be paying at a higher interest rate and your loan may only extend over a very short time.
- ☐ You want to rearrange an endowment mortgage and your present lender can't or won't do this.
- ☐ You had a mortgage from your last employer who offered you a cut-price interest rate, but you have now lost your job or want to change it.
- ☐ You had a bridging loan from your bank to help you buy your home and you now have to repay it.

Who can you ask for a new mortgage?

You should ask a building society or your local authority, because they usually lend at the cheapest rate. Both lend money for housing purposes. If one of your present loans was used for some other purpose they may be reluctant to help you, but very often both will have the power to help. Building societies' wide powers to lend money against the security of property are given under Section 10 of the Building Societies Act 1986. Although societies lend money to buy, improve or repair property they can make secured or unsecured loans for other reasons. Local authorities' power to lend is given under Section 435 of the Housing Act 1985, Part XIV. This section gives authorities the power to lend for buying, constructing, converting, improving or repairing homes, and also to repay previous loans taken out for any of the above purposes. You can try approaching your local authority for a mortgage under this Section.

Depending on the circumstances, local authorities may refuse a new mortgage if one of the present loans was taken out for non-housing purposes. Ask your building society for a new mortgage if you have your first mortgage with that society. Ask your local authority for a new mortgage if your first mortgage is with that local authority.

If your local authority cannot help you with a new mortgage themselves they may be able to help by referring you to a local building society under the Support Scheme.

Don't ask a finance company to give you a new mortgage, because their expensive loan could land you in even more trouble.

How much are you likely to get?

If you are working: Different lenders have different ways of calculating how much they will lend to someone with your income. The lenders will multiply your gross annual income by a certain figure, and this figure may change when interest rates change.

Example:
Jim Smith earns £8,000 a year and his wife earns £5,000. Their lender's policy is to multiply his gross income by two and a half times and to add on one times her gross income. They could hope to get a new mortgage for £25,000, ie, (£8,000 × 2.5 = £20,000) plus (£5,000 × 1 = £5,000).

You may be able to get more than this if you need it. You will have to show exactly how you will meet the new payments out of your present income. (Check the amount of your new payments with Appendix 2).

If you are not working and are receiving income support: You will have to show the lender that your social security office will meet all or part of the interest payments on the amount you need for the new mortgage. For more information on this, see page 47.

How to negotiate with your lenders

There are two steps to take. First, you must find out how much you owe on your second and later mortgages. Second, you must ask your first lender for a new mortgage to cover all your debts, including, of course, the first mortgage and any arrears on that loan.

Write to all your lenders, other than the first, stating:

- ☐ your name, address and mortgage account number;
- ☐ that you want to pay back (or redeem) your loans;
- ☐ that you want a **redemption figure**. (This is the amount you still owe your lender. It will include the capital you have not yet paid back and any arrears.) The figure may be higher than you

expect, both because some companies charge interest on arrears and because some charge a fee for allowing you to redeem before the end of the term. If you think that the fee is unreasonably high, do not just accept it. Get advice from your local consumer advice centre or one of the agencies listed in Appendix 10.

Remember to keep a copy of this letter.

Write to the lender from whom you want a new mortgage stating:

- ☐ your name, address and mortgage account number (if you already have an account with that lender);
- ☐ that you will need an amount to cover all present loans, including your first mortgage. Give the redemption figures that you have received from other lenders, stating the month to which they apply;
- ☐ your present total income. This should include your gross income (before any deductions), that of any members of your family living with you, and all the benefits you get, such as child benefit, family credit, rate rebate, income support, housing benefit and national insurance benefits;
- ☐ that you have calculated you will be able to manage the new mortgage payments (see Appendix 2) as well as your other commitments . Show that you have considered costs such as travelling to work and child-minding.

Remember to keep a copy of this letter.

You must check the redemption figures with the other companies when you know the date on which the new mortgage will be granted. This is because the figures may change from month to month, depending on how many more payments you make and on whether the rate of interest changes. If the redemption figures do go up, you will have to ask your new lender to cover this increase.

APPEALS TO LENDERS

All building societies now have an internal complaints procedure as required by the Building Societies Act 1986. If you are dissatisfied with any decision your building society has made about your loan you can ask to be referred through this procedure.

If you are still dissatisfied with the outcome of the internal complaints procedure you can refer your case to the Building Societies Ombudsman Scheme. You should contact the Ombudsman's office if you believe your building society has treated you unfairly, been guilty of maladministration (including inefficiency or undue delay) in a way that results in you losing money or suffering inconvenience. If s/he can deal with your complaint s/he will see if it is possible to negotiate a settlement. If that fails s/he will make his/her own impartial decision as to who is right.

Either phone the Ombudsman's office (01-931-0044) for a complaint form or write to The Office of the Building Societies' Ombudsman, 35-37 Grosvenor Gardens, London SW1X 7AW.

Anyone applying to the local authority for a mortgage can ask their local councillor for help in changing an unfavourable decision. Your local town hall or library can give you the names of your ward councillors. Additionally, if you feel the local authority have treated you unfairly or discriminated against you, you can ask your local councillor to refer your case to the Ombudsman. The Local Ombudsman is independent and can investigate complaints against local authorities.

If you have borrowed money from any other source and are having difficulties, it is worth writing to their head office just in case the decision can be reversed.

CHAPTER THREE

How to increase your income if you or your partner are working 24 hours or more each week

Besides trying to cut your mortgage costs, you should also see if there are ways of increasing your weekly income. This chapter explains the extra benefits you should think about claiming for yourself and/or your family if you or your partner are working 24 hours or more each week. If you are already claiming these benefits, use this chapter to check that you are getting the right amounts. The figures given are correct for the period between April 1988 and April 1989. You may find that you are not quite sure whether you qualify for some of the benefits. The best advice is, if in doubt, claim. You lose nothing by applying, and the extra money you gain may make the difference between being able to stay in your home and having to sell because you cannot pay the mortgage.

FAMILY CREDIT

Family credit (FC) is a new weekly cash payment intended to help families on low wages. It can amount to a substantial sum each week, and you may be surprised at how much income you can have and still get some FC. For example, a family with two teenage children at school might have an income of almost £140 per week and still get some FC. (See Appendix 3 for a guide to whether you qualify.) When a man and woman living together as a couple apply for FC, the woman must make the claim (unless the Secretary of State decides, in a specific case, that it would be reasonable to accept the claim from the man). However, both parties will have to sign the claim form.

You can claim FC if you, or your partner:

- ☐ have one or more dependent children under 19;
- ☐ normally work at least 24 hours a week. This includes any paid meal breaks, and can be made up from more than one part-time job;
- ☐ have less than £6,000 in savings or other capital.

In assessing how much capital you have the DHSS will take into account money in a bank or building society, savings certificates, shares and property amongst other things. Some capital will be ignored, however, including life insurance and endowment policies, and the value of the home you live in. If you own, or partly own, a home that you no longer live in (eg, because of a divorce or separation), you should get advice from one of the organisations listed in Appendix 10. For more details about the capital rules, see Appendix 6.

How and when to claim

Get the DHSS leaflet FC1 from your local post office or nearest social security office. It includes the claim form and a return envelope. If you can't get the leaflet easily, write to your local social security office and say that you want to claim FC—or ring Freephone 0800-666555 and ask them to send you a claim form. There is no charge for the call.

If there are no complications, you will receive an order book back by post and it will last for 26 weeks starting from the Tuesday after you signed the form. You then cash the book each week at the post office, or you can ask for it to be paid directly into your bank or building society account. Once issued, a book cannot usually be altered, so if your situation changes for the better, you can still keep cashing your book. On the other hand, if your income goes down during the year, your FC will not be increased. FC was intended to be easy to claim, and generally it is. Check below, however, to make sure you remember to include everything when you fill in the form.

- ☐ Your wage has to be checked. You are asked to send your last 5 wage slips or last 2 monthly salary slips. FC can only be backdated in very limited circumstances, ie, you must be able to show that you had good reason for claiming late. (See below for what may count as 'good cause' for a late claim.) Don't delay claiming if you don't have your wage slips. Write on the form that you will send them later. If you do have details, you will probably need them for claiming other benefits, so try and get a photocopy made and send that instead of the original. If you have only just started a job, then the DHSS will ask your employer to estimate what your earnings are likely to be over the next 5 weeks.

- ☐ Your most recent wages may have been higher than usual. This could be because of extra overtime or seasonal work. If so, write on the form that you want an earlier and more normal period to be used in assessing your eligibility to claim FC; say what the period is and give details of your gross income at that time.
- ☐ You may have been paid more in the recent past than you are earning now and expect to earn in the next year. This could be because you have just cut down your hours of work, or you have changed your job and are getting a lower wage. If so, state on the form that you want FC to be awarded on the basis of your earnings as at the date of your claim because these now represent your normal earnings (explain why). Offer to send them your wage slips for the next five weeks when you get them. Seek advice if the DHSS refuse to award you FC on this basis (see Appendix 10).
- ☐ You may be receiving maintenance payments which arrive irregularly, or not at all. If this happens, the DHSS should take an average of the payments you have received in the last 13 weeks before your claim, and treat that as your normal income.
- ☐ Capital or savings below £3,000 do not affect FC. Any savings or capital between £3,000 and £6,000 are treated as giving you an assumed income of £1 per week for each £250 (or part of £250) that you have over £3,000. For example, savings of £3,500 would be treated as giving you an income of £2 per week. This is known as **tariff income**.
- ☐ If you think you should have been receiving FC before now, your claim can be backdated for up to a year, provided you had 'good cause' for not claiming before. Ignorance of your right to make a claim is not generally considered to be 'good cause'. However, if you had good reason to believe that you were not

entitled, this may be 'good cause'. For example, you will have 'good cause' for claiming late if you were wrongly advised by the DHSS, or by a solicitor. You may wish to get advice about this in which case, see Appendix 10 for details of where to go for help.

- ☐ You may include in your claim children who are members of your household and for whom you claim child benefit. Children who spend time away from home, for instance, because they are in care, may still be members of your household if they return regularly and often.
- ☐ If you, or your partner's hours of work fluctuate, the DHSS will take an average, to check that they add up to at least 24 hours a week. If there is a regular cycle (eg, a monthly shift rota), then an average will be taken over the period of that cycle. If there is no pattern, the DHSS will use the last 5 weeks, or any other appropriate period.

How much will you receive?

This depends on how much your net weekly income is over a certain amount, known as the 'threshold', which is fixed by parliament each year. (It is £51.45 until April 1989.) If your net income is below this threshold, then you receive an amount known as 'maximum family credit'. This amount varies according to the number and ages of your children. As your income rises above the threshold, your maximum FC is reduced by 70 pence in the pound. So if your net income is £10 over the threshold, your maximum FC would be reduced by £7. See Appendix 3 for details of the calculation.

How to calculate your net weekly income

First, take your full weekly earnings before any deductions, then subtract the tax, national insurance, and half of any superannuation contributions. This is the figure used as your **net earnings**. If you are a couple, both incomes will be counted.

Second, add to this figure any maintenance and national insurance benefits you receive, but do not include any of the following: child benefit, one parent benefit, housing benefit, attendance allowance, mobility allowance, fostering allowances, educational maintenance allowances, or money paid by grown-up sons, daughters or lodgers for their keep, or, unless you have been receiving either statutory sick pay or statutory maternity pay for more than 13 weeks.

If you are self-employed, your net profit over the previous year is usually used to work out your income, although a more recent period can be used if that would be a better reflection of your normal earnings.

Example:
(This example uses the benefit rates for April 1988 to April 1989.)

Mr Rider is a messenger earning £80 net per week. His wife works part-time in a supermarket and earns £20 net per week. They have three children aged 13, 9, and 7. Their combined weekly net income is £100. This is £48.55 over the family credit 'threshold' of £51.45. The maximum family credit for their family is £55.60 (see Appendix 3 for details of this).

Their family credit is worked out by taking 70 pence in the pound of the amount their income is over the threshold (ie, 70 per cent of £48.55 = £33.98) away from the maximum family credit for their family:

£55.60 – £33.98 = £21.62 family credit

Timing your claim for family credit

A family already receiving FC at the time of the April increases will not receive the increase until their current award runs out and they re-apply. For example, if the FC award started in December 1988 the family would not benefit from the new rates until their current award ran out after 26 weeks, in June 1989, and they claimed once more.

If you are thinking of claiming FC in February or March, it may, in some circumstances, be worth delaying your claim until April because you may be better off overall by foregoing benefit for a few weeks, then qualifying for 6 months at the higher rate. In the same way, it may be worth considering whether your circumstances are about to change in ways that might lead to a higher amount of FC. For example, if you are about to take a drop in income, or have another child.

You may want to discuss the merits of delaying a claim with an advice agency (see Appendix 10).

If you are not satisfied with the decision on your claim

You can appeal within 3 months of the date of the decision if you are refused FC or feel you have not received the right amount. You will then be able to put your case to a local tribunal, but you should get advice about this before you go. See Appendix 10 for where to get help.

Claim family credit however small your entitlement

It is always worth getting FC, even if the weekly amount is the lowest possible, that is 50 pence. This is because you will only need to show your FC book to receive other benefits free for all the family, including hospital fares, prescriptions, optical vouchers and dental treatment. You may also get free or reduced cost legal help under the Legal Aid Scheme and reduced price powdered milk if you have a child under 1 year old.

RATE REBATES

A rate rebate results in your paying less general (not water and sewerage) rates to your local authority. It is part of the housing benefit scheme administered by your local authority. To qualify you, together with your partner if you have one, must have less than £8,000 in capital and savings. (See Appendix 6 for details of what is taken into account when making this assessment). However low your income, the highest rebate you can get is 80 per cent of your general rates.

Special note for separated wives/cohabitees: you may be paying the rates on your house, even though your ex-partner is the person liable for them. In this case, the local authority can still pay you a rebate, so long as it considers it 'reasonable' to treat you as eligible. This rule is found in Regulation 6 of the Housing Benefit Regulations. If the local authority refuses you a rebate see Appendix 10 for details of where you can get advice.

How to claim a rebate

Fill in a rebate form which you can get from either the housing or the finance department of your local authority. Don't delay claiming if you do not have wage slips or proof of any savings handy as you could miss out on some rebate. Your rebate is usually worked out from the date you apply, but you can ask for payments for earlier months if you have a good reason for applying late (see below). You will not be visited at home or have to go for an interview, but do remember that you have to let the local authority know whenever your circumstances change, for example if your income goes up or down or if someone leaves or joins the household.

When you put in an application for rate rebate the local authority is under a legal duty to decide your claim within 14 days of receiving all the information it needs. This deadline can only be exceeded if it is not 'reasonably practicable' for the authority to decide your claim within the time limit. (This is laid down by Regulation 76 of the Housing Benefit Regulations.)

Authorities are warned in a DHSS circular that exceeding the 14-day time limit should be the exception to the general rule.

If you think you should have been receiving a rebate for some time, you can ask for your claim to be backdated. However, this will only be done if you can show that you have had 'good cause' for not claiming before now (see page 22 for a discussion of the same rule for FC). An example of 'good cause' might be if a woman thought that her ex-husband was paying the rates and then discovered that he hadn't been. It is a good idea to get advice about this from one of the organisations listed in Appendix 10. A rebate cannot be backdated by more than 52 weeks.

Any award of rate rebate will last for a set period. You will then have to re-apply, but if your circumstances have not changed you don't have to give the same information all over again. If the award was for more than a 4-month period the local authority must send you a reminder to claim again before the period expires. To avoid any gap in benefit you must re-apply within a month of the award expiring.

The rebate calculation

This depends on four things: your income, your rates, the number and ages of people in your family, and whether anyone else lives in your house, eg, lodgers, or grown-up sons or daughters. The calculation works by comparing your net income with the 'applicable amount' for your family. This is worked out from calculations based on the size and circumstances of your family. If your income is the same, or lower than your **applicable amount**, you will receive **maximum housing benefit**, which is usually 80 per cent of your rates. As your income goes over the **applicable amount**, your rebate is reduced.

The rebate application form will ask you for all the details necessary for this calculation. However, here are some points to watch out for.

- ☐ Remember to tell the local authority if you are making maintenance payments to a former family. These amounts will be ignored when calculating your income.

- ☐ Tell the local authority if you are supposed to be receiving maintenance but it is not being paid. The law says your rebate should be based on what your income is, or is likely to be, and not what it might be if you received the maintenance due.

- ☐ If you have a person staying with you who is not your partner, or a dependent child (under 16, or under 19 if still in full-time secondary education), your rebate may be reduced as that person (called officially a 'non-dependant') is expected to contribute towards your rates. See page 48 to find out how much the reduction (if any) is likely to be. Remember that you must let the local authority know if a non-dependant moves in or out of your home, as this affects how much your rebate will be.

- ☐ Make sure you tell the local authority if you or your partner used to receive invalidity benefit or severe disablement allowance, but are now receiving a retirement pension or widow's pension instead, or if you have been unfit for work for more than 28 weeks. It could mean that you get a larger rebate.

- ☐ If the local authority considers that your rates are unreasonably high, compared with other suitable homes, or that your home is unreasonably large for your needs, they can base the rebate calculation on a lower rates figure. However this power should not be used very often, and in many cases should only be used if it would be reasonable to expect you to move. If the local authority reduces your rebate in this way, get advice from one of the organisations listed in Appendix 10.

- ☐ You can check the calculation of your rebate by asking for a detailed statement of the assessment. Local authorities must provide a detailed statement of how your rebate has been calculated within 14 days of being asked, unless this is 'not reasonably practicable'. (This rule is laid down in Regulation 80 of the Housing Benefit Regulations.) The local advice centres mentioned in Appendix 10 might be able to go through the statement with you.

If you are unhappy about the amount of your rebate, you have a right to ask the local authority to review its decision within 6 weeks of your being notified of it. If you are still dissatisfied, you have 28 days to ask for a further review by a review board. You can get further advice on how to challenge a local authority's decision concerning your rate rebate from the organisations listed in Appendix 10.

The local authority can pay you a higher amount of housing benefit if it considers that your circumstances are 'exceptional'. This power is not used very often, but you should argue for a higher amount of housing benefit if you would otherwise be in hardship. For example, you may have extra costs due to an illness or disability, but not meet the very strict conditions for the disability premium. You should ask the local authority to pay this extra benefit under regulation 69. For advice or assistance on this, see Appendix 10.

OTHER WAYS OF REDUCING YOUR RATES

Under Section 53 of the General Rate Act 1967, the local authority has the power to reduce or cancel completely the rates due from anyone experiencing 'poverty'. You could argue for this power to be used if you have built up arrears of rates over a time when you could have claimed a rebate, or if you are unable to manage the rates for some other reason. You may need help from an advice agency or local councillor to persuade the local authority to use this power.

It is also possible to get rate relief if you, or one of your family, are disabled and there are special facilities in your house to meet their needs. These might include: an extra bathroom or toilet; a room used mainly by a disabled person; a garage or parking space; or central heating. The house does not have to have been specially adapted, it is only necessary for the special feature to be important for the disabled person's wellbeing. You can get more information about this from the rates department of the local authority.

IF YOU WERE WORKING 24-29 HOURS A WEEK BEFORE APRIL 1988

If you, or your partner, were working 24-29 hours a week, and were getting supplementary benefit before 11 April 1988, you will have lost your benefit when the new income support scheme was introduced. This is because the income support rules say that you cannot claim benefit if either you or your partner work 24 hours a week or more.

In May 1988, the government changed the rules to allow some people who lost benefit because of this '24-hour rule' to keep their old level of benefit after all. These changes may affect the following groups of people:

— families with children;
— widows;
— pensioners;
— some disabled people.

If you think you may fit into one of these categories, you should ring the DHSS (Freeline 0800-393555) or write to them at: DHSS (Transitional Payments), FREEPOST, PO Box 462, Glasgow G40 1BR; or get DHSS leaflet SB22 from your local social security office.

HELP WITH YOUR POLL TAX (COMMUNITY CHARGE)

In April 1989 in Scotland, rates will be replaced by the community charge, or poll tax as it is otherwise known. A rebate scheme is due to be introduced which will probably be very similar to the present rate rebate system. For more details, readers in Scotland should contact their local authority, or one of the agencies listed in Appendix 10.

BENEFITS FOR YOUR CHILDREN

Child benefit

Child benefit is a tax free payment of £7.25 per week per child. It will be paid four-weekly in arrears *unless* you choose to be paid weekly. You can do this if you are in receipt of FC or one parent benefit (see below) or income support (see Chapter Four). You can also be paid weekly if monthly payment is causing you hardship—for example, you are on a low income, or have a large family and prefer weekly payments to help you budget. You ask for weekly payments by writing to the Child Benefit Centre, PO Box 1, Newcastle-upon-Tyne, NE88 1AA.

You will get child benefit for every child under 16, or under 19 and still in secondary education. When your child leaves school or college and is still under 19, you continue to receive child benefit until the end of the school holiday after the term in which they leave, ie, until the first Monday in September, the first Monday in January or the first Monday after Easter Monday. However, you will not get child benefit during that final holiday period for any week your child is working full-time (including a holiday job) or is on a Training Commission course.

From September 1988, the period that child benefit is paid for 16- and 17-year-old school leavers is being extended. It will be paid for an extra 12 weeks for Christmas and Easter leavers, and 16 weeks for 16- and 17-year-olds who leave in the summer. Child benefit will continue to be paid during this period, provided the young person is registered for work or a YTS place, unless the 16- or 17- year-old gets a full-time job (24 hours or more), or starts on a YTS course. In most cases, 16- and 17-year-olds will no longer be able to claim any benefits in their own right if they are unemployed. For more detailed advice about when 16- or 17- year-olds may still be able to claim, contact one of the organisations listed in Appendix 10.

How to claim

Ask for a form at a post office or social security office, and send it to the Child Benefit Centre (address above). You will then get an order book to cash at the post office.

Points to note

Your claim for child benefit is assessed at the Child Benefit Centre in Newcastle. If your claim is not allowed, you can appeal against the decision by writing to the adjudication officer at your local social security office. You will then be able to put your case to a local tribunal. But you should get advice first. See Appendix 10 for who you should go to for help.

One parent benefit

This is an additional benefit payable on top of child benefit to people bringing up children on their own. You only get one addition of £4.90, irrespective of how many children you have. Although called 'one parent benefit', it can be paid to people other than the parents. But one parent benefit is not paid if you receive certain other benefits for your child—eg, additions to widow's benefit. You claim one parent benefit by filling in the claim form contained in DHSS leaflet CH11. Your claim can be backdated for up to 6 months. A married person who has separated can claim once s/he is legally separated *or* when separation has lasted at least 13 weeks and is likely to be permanent. An unmarried parent can claim one parent benefit from the point of separation from a partner, if the separation is likely to be permanent.

School clothing

Some local authorities give grants for school uniform and for other items of clothing and footwear your children may need. Apply to the local education office. The amount you receive may vary considerably and so does the level of income below which you qualify, the number of grants you can have in any one year, and the way you receive them. You may find that you get a voucher that you have to exchange at one particular shop. If you cannot get all you need at that shop, you may then have to wait for another voucher to be made out for a different shop. This could mean weeks of delay, so do claim in good time before term begins. You could also contact local authority councillors and try to encourage them to improve the local scheme or introduce one, if the local authority doesn't operate one at present.

Study grants for children over 16

If your child stays on at school, you may qualify for an educational maintenance allowance from your local authority. Again, the amount varies. Educational Maintenance Allowances do not affect your benefit at all, if you receive family credit or rate rebate. There is a similar grant, called a minor award, for children who leave school but go full-time to a technical college. Claim at the education office.

School fares

If you have children under 8 who travel more than 2 miles to school, or children over 8 who travel more than 3 miles, you should claim free passes for them from your local authority. This is the general rule, but each authority also has the power to pay any other fare that seems reasonable. You might get help if, say, your child has to travel just less than the stated distances, or if the increased cost of fares creates a special difficulty for you.

HEALTH BENEFITS

Family credit gives you automatic entitlement to the following benefits for yourself and your family: free prescriptions, dental treatment, optical vouchers, refunds of fares to hospital for treatment, reduced prices for powdered milk if you have a child under one year old.

Children under 16 qualify automatically for free prescriptions. Dental care is free for all under-18-year-olds and for people in full-time education under 19. People under 19 who are still in full-time education can also get certain types of glasses free. In addition, you and any teenage children may receive free health benefits on grounds of low income. Ask at your local DHSS office or post office for form AG1.

Points to note

- ☐ If in doubt, claim.
- ☐ If you do not qualify for help with prescriptions, you may save

money by buying a prescription 'season ticket'. At present, this costs £13.50 for 4 months or £37.50 a year. If you need more than 5 items in the next 4 months, or more than 15 in the next year, you will save money. Get a claim form from a post office or social security office.

INCOME TAX FOR SEPARATED PARTNERS

Although your tax position may change on separation, if you have, or are about to split up, *your tax code will not be altered unless you let your tax office know what has happened*. You should see to this straightaway. As it is the woman left in the home who has most problems with tax, her situation is discussed in this section. The current levels of tax allowance are set out in Appendix 1.

- ☐ **Unmarried partners:** the tax system takes no account of people who live together as husband and wife but who are not legally married. Therefore, if you and your partner separate and you are not married to one another that will not, by itself, affect your tax position.
- ☐ **A separated husband** continues to be treated as a married man for tax purposes for the rest of the tax year during which he separates from his wife. After that, he may keep the married man's personal allowance, but only if he is making voluntary payments to his wife. A voluntary payment is one that is not made under a court order or under a legally enforceable agreement between the couple, for example, a deed of separation.
- ☐ **A separated wife** will find that things are not quite so straightforward. You will be taxed as a single person from the month you separate, and will then have to claim any extra allowances to which you are entitled. Simply write to your tax office, and ask to claim the allowances listed below. Your employer will be able to give you the address of your tax office.

The additional personal allowance

You can claim the additional personal allowance if you are bringing up a child on your own. The child must be living with you. This allowance brings your own single person's allowance up to the same amount as a married man's personal allowance.

The single person's and working wife's allowance

If you separate from your husband, you are entitled to the *whole* of the single person's allowance from the date of separation, until the following April. *In addition* you can claim the whole of the wife's earned income allowance from the beginning of the previous tax year until the date of separation, to set against any earned income you have. For example, if you are earning £60 per week between April and September you could set the whole year's wife's earned income allowance against this. If you left your husband in September, you would then have the whole of the single person's allowance to set against the income earned between then and the next April.

Mortgage tax relief

Most people no longer need to claim mortgage tax relief, because they receive their tax relief automatically in the form of reduced repayments to the lender. This arrangement is called MIRAS and is explained on page 10. As a separated wife, you will only need to apply for tax relief on the mortgage if it is outside the MIRAS scheme—eg, because you have to pay tax at more than the standard rate. From 6 April 1987, even most of *these* loans will automatically be subject to tax relief.

Maintenance

You will need to sort out what maintenance payments are due to you, and how they will be paid.

- ☐ **Is the payment voluntary?**
  If your husband pays you maintenance as a result of an informal agreement, that money is completely disregarded for tax purposes. He cannot claim tax relief on what he pays you, and you will not be taxed on what you receive.

- ☐ **If the payment is not voluntary, how is the court order worded for your children's payments?**
  It is best to have the court order state that maintenance for your children is to be paid *to* each child and not to you *for* each child. This is because the money to your child counts as your child's income and not as yours. It will, therefore, be left out of the calculation of your tax bill if the total annual maintenance paid to

each child is below the single person's tax allowance. See Appendix 1 for the current figure. You should ask your solicitor to bear this in mind when you are deciding on maintenance and you should ask for the court order to be re-phrased if it has already been made. This arrangement will not affect your husband's tax position at all. But for you it will be an important way of making sure that you pay no more tax than you need to.

☐ **What is the amount awarded by the court for each person?** The treatment of maintenance varies according to the amount to be paid and the person who is to receive it.

If the maintenance is 'for' a child under 21 and it is £18 or less per week (£78 per month), or 'to' a child under 21 or for you and is £33 or less per week (£143 per month), your husband should pay the full amount stated on the court order. He can then claim tax relief on those payments. The maintenance you receive will count as part of your taxable income.

If the maintenance is 'for' a child under 21 and is *more than* £18 per week, or 'to' a child under 21 or for you and is *more than* £33 per week, your husband does not have to pay you the full amount stated on the court order. He will deduct tax from the sum at the standard rate (currently 25 per cent) and pay you the rest (ie, 75 per cent at current rates).

He should also give you a form R185 which says how much tax has been deducted. You should then give the Inland Revenue form R185. You will not have to pay any more tax on the money, unless you are in a higher tax bracket. Also, if you do not have to pay tax at all because your annual income is less than your allowances, you will be able to get a tax refund from your tax inspector.

There can be problems where the payer refuses to supply form R185. Although the payer has to supply the form by law, the Inland Revenue says it recognises that taking the person to court is not always possible. In these circumstances, the tax inspector is advised to consider other evidence of tax deductions, such as bank statements, cleared cheques or correspondence.

Note: For maintenance orders made after 15 March 1988, tax relief is only available on payments of up to £1,490 each year. Unmarried parents paying maintenance are no longer eligible for any tax relief on new orders. Maintenance orders made before 15 March 1988 are unaffected by this new legislation certainly until April 1989. For more information on this, contact your local tax office, or one of the agencies listed in Appendix 10.

☐ **Does your maintenance arrive regularly?**
If your maintenance fluctuates, you may end up paying tax on money you have yet to receive. You can prevent this happening in the future by having your wages and your maintenance for the current year taxed separately. Ask the tax office to set all your personal allowances against your pay from work and, at the same time, ask for your maintenance to be taxed 'under Schedule D'. You will then pay tax on your wages in the normal way. But, halfway through the tax year, you will get a tax bill relating to your maintenance for that year. You can ask for payment to be deferred until the end of the tax year when you are certain how much maintenance you have received in the course of the year. At the end of the year, you can then ask to pay the tax bill in instalments, rather than as a lump sum, to relieve hardship. One suggestion is to ask to pay the tax for the previous year through the PAYE system.

Other problems

☐ **Backdated claims:** You may have realised that you have not claimed all the allowances you could have since you separated. Don't panic. You can ask for a reassessment of the tax you have paid during the last 6 years.

☐ **Inaccessible tax office:** You may need to discuss your case with a tax inspector, but find that your tax matters are dealt with by an office at the other end of the country. You can ask for your papers to be sent to an office in your area and arrange a personal interview with an inspector there.

☐ **If you stop work:** You may decide to stop work and stay at home to look after your children. See Chapter Four for details about income support. You should let your tax office know and claim a tax rebate. Make a claim immediately. If you wait until the end of the tax year before making your claim, the process of checking and sending your rebate will be much longer. If you stop work and are unemployed (ie, you are 'signing on' at the unemployment benefit office), you will not be able to claim your tax rebate until you start work again or until the end of the tax year, whichever comes first.

CHAPTER FOUR

How to increase your income if you and your partner are not working or are working less than 24 hours a week

You may have been told that, because your family circumstances have changed, you cannot afford to stay on in your home and that you should sell up and move out. It may be that you are sick, have been made redundant, have only part-time work or have been left by your partner. If you want to keep your home, advice to sell and move can sometimes be disastrously wrong and you should never do this without first looking at all the possible ways of staying where you are.

INCOME SUPPORT

Most of this chapter is concerned with **income support**. This is the main benefit for people not working or where they and their partner each work less than 24 hours per week. It can be paid on its own or to 'top up' other income you have, such as sick pay or unemployment benefit, although these benefits will be taken into account in assessing your total weekly income. If you have to depend on income support for some, or all, of your weekly income, this does not mean that you will have to give up your home. Income support can be a very stable income and increases at least once a year. In most cases, you will be able to get payment for some or all of the interest portion of your mortgage, and you may be able to repay the capital as well. Don't worry if you think your outgoings are too high; most people can cut these costs in one of the ways described in Chapter Two.

If your income is too high you may not qualify for income support. See page 57 for other benefits to claim.

Who can claim

Any person aged 18 or over whose weekly income is below a certain level may claim income support. There are a number of exceptions to this general rule. The main ones are that you cannot claim income support if:

- ☐ either you or your partner work 24 hours or more a week;
- ☐ you and your partner have capital and savings of more than £6,000.

To work out how much capital you have the DHSS will take into account things like money in a bank or building society, savings certificates, shares and property. However, some capital will be ignored including life insurance and endowment policies, and the value of the home in which you live. If you own, or partly own, a home in which you no longer live (eg, because of a divorce or separation) you should get advice from one of the organisations listed in Appendix 10. For more details about the capital rules, see Appendix 6.

Special note for separated partners: If you leave the home you own or jointly own because of a breakdown in your relationship, your share of the value of the house will be ignored for at least 26 weeks when calculating how much capital you have. If you make efforts to sell the home, or take legal action to allow you to move back into the house, then it can be ignored for longer. See Appendix 6 for more details.

Some people aged 16-17 can claim income support but only in very limited circumstances. Many claimants of income support have to sign on at the unemployment benefit office in order to receive benefit. There are, however, many groups of people who need not sign on, including single parents with children under 16; those unable to work because they are ill or because they are looking after a severely disabled person; and people aged 60 or over.

Only one partner can claim on behalf of a couple. You can choose which of you makes the claim, but if one of you is too ill or disabled to work, then it is often best for that person to be the claimant. It may mean that you get more income support. It is possible to swap the claimant role between partners.

These rules apply to both married and unmarried couples.

A man and a woman will be treated as a couple by the DHSS if it is thought they are 'living together as husband and wife'. This is sometimes known as the 'cohabitation rule'. The DHSS may say that you are cohabiting when you do not agree that you are. You should appeal if this means that your income support is withdrawn or your claim refused. For advice on this, you could contact one of the organisations listed in Appendix 10.

How and when to claim

You should claim immediately if you think that you might be entitled to income support, since you cannot normally get payment for a period before you claim.

Income support can only be backdated where you can show 'good cause' for your claim being late. This means that you have a good reason why you did not claim earlier. Ignorance of your entitlement is not sufficient. However, if your belief that you were not entitled is a reasonable one given the circumstances, that can be 'good cause'. For example, you will have 'good cause' for claiming late if you were wrongly advised by the DHSS or by a solicitor. You may wish to seek advice about this—see Appendix 10.

- ☐ **If you do have to sign on**, you claim income support by going to the local unemployment benefit office and asking for form B1. This is a detailed questionnaire, which you should fill in and either send to the address you will be given or hand into a special counter in the office. Form B1 also includes a separate form to claim a rate rebate (housing benefit) from the local authority. The adjudication officer, having seen the information you give on form B1, will decide whether you qualify for income support and, if so, how much. If you have children, you may be visited by the DHSS at some point during the 3 months following your claim. The visiting officer comes to check you are getting the correct amount of benefit. You will be asked to produce various documents which confirm the information you gave on form B1—eg, details of your mortgage repayments, bank statements, savings books, child benefit order books and details of any other income you have.
- ☐ **If you do not have to sign on**, contact your local DHSS office. You will find the address under 'H' (for Health and Social Security) in the 'phonebook. You could telephone them and ask to claim, but it is safer to write and keep a dated copy of

□ your letter. You need not write in detail as the DHSS will send you a full questionnaire (see below). If you need money urgently, it is probaby best to visit the office immediately.

Once they hear from you, the DHSS should send you a detailed claim form. This form asks you to state all your personal details so that the DHSS can work out if you are entitled and, if so, to how much. Be sure to tell them everything. If you have reading or writing problems, or some other good reason why you would rather explain your circumstances to a DHSS officer than fill in a form (eg, your claim is complex or you need money quickly), let the DHSS know and they should arrange for you to come to their offices for an interview, or send someone out to visit you. They will also arrange an interview if the information you put on the form needs clarification.

Be prepared for an interview or visit by collecting together all the documents which might be relevant to your claim—eg, statements about mortgages on your house, details of any savings including bank statements or building society books, maintenance agreements or orders, child benefit order books, and details of any other income you have. It is a good idea to write out a statement of your situation to hand in at the interview if you have not already written a full account of your position in a letter or on the appropriate forms.

How payment is made

If you are entitled to income support, the date you will first be paid benefit depends on what other benefit(s) you may already be receiving. Most pensioners are paid weekly in advance—normally on a Monday. Most other people, except people signing unemployed, are paid weekly in arrears. People who sign unemployed are usually paid fortnightly in arrears.

You will be sent form A14N with a brief breakdown of how your benefit is calculated. You can ask to be sent a fuller form, called A124, which gives a much more comprehensive breakdown of your benefit assessment. You can use this to check your benefit against pages 41-54 in this Guide. At the same time as telling you about your income support entitlement, the DHSS should send the rate rebate form you filled in at the same time as the income support form to the local authority. They will confirm to the local authority that you are receiving income support.

See page 55 for more information about rate rebates.

How income support works

Most decisions on claims for income support are taken by officials known as adjudication officers. The adjudication officer decides your case according to the Social Security Act 1986 and regulations made under that Act. These are highly detailed and sometimes very complex. The current Act and regulations are kept in a loose-leaf book called *The Law Relating to Social Security*, also known as the 'Blue Book', which you can inspect at any local DHSS office. Larger reference libraries should also have a copy. Whilst this Guide gives a broad picture of the income support scheme as it affects owner occupiers, for a more detailed guide to the rules governing the income support system, see CPAG's *National Welfare Benefits Handbook* (Appendix 11).

Because the income support scheme is so complicated, you should not just rely on the DHSS to calculate your benefit correctly. You may not have received all the premiums to which you are entitled, or the adjudication officer might have made a mistake about the regulations. If you are dissatisfied with an adjudication officer's decision, you can appeal to a local tribunal (see page 55). Appendix 10 suggests places you can go to get further advice about your benefit entitlements.

How much will you receive

The adjudication officer will work out your **applicable amount** (what the law says you need to live on each week) and your **income** (the money you have coming in each week). If your income is less than the applicable amount, you will be awarded income support to make up the difference. If your applicable amount is more than your income, you will not get any income support (but see page 57 for details of other benefits you may be able to claim). Here's how your applicable amount and income will be calculated.

Your applicable amount

Your applicable amount is divided up into three parts (see Appendix 5 for the rates until April 1989):

(i) **Personal Allowances** cover the day-to-day living expenses for you, your partner and any dependent children. The amounts are set by parliament each year, and usually go up in April. The amounts for your children vary according to their ages. You get a lower rate of benefit if you are single and under 25 (without children), and a lower amount still if you are eligible for income support under 18. Couples where both partners are under 18 also get a lower allowance.

(ii) **Premiums** are standard additional amounts paid to particular groups of people. There are premiums for: families with children; pensioners; single parents; disabled people; the severely disabled; and disabled children. The pensioner, higher pensioner and disability premiums are all paid at either a single or a couple rate. Normally only one premium can be paid at a time, and you will receive the highest one you are entitled to. Exceptions to this are: the family premium, which is paid on top of any other premium; the disabled child premium, where one premium is paid for each disabled child, on top of any other premium; and the severe disability premium, which can be paid on top of the disability or higher pensioner premiums. Appendix 5 gives more details of who can get each premium.

(iii) **Housing costs** that can be met from income support include:

☐ **Mortgage interest payments.** Usually the DHSS can only pay the interest on the mortgage or loan taken out to buy the home. However, they can pay the interest on a second mortgage, or a new mortgage which is paying off an earlier one on the same property. Separated partners can get other second mortgages paid (see special note below). However, there are a number of common situations in which less than the whole amount of the interest will be paid (see page 47).

☐ **Interest on loans for repairs and improvements**. To qualify, loans do not have to be secured on the house, and can be for 'major repairs necessary to maintain the fabric of the dwelling', as well as for improvements such as damp proofing, the installation of central heating, and double glazing. See page 67 for a complete list.

Note that the DHSS will not pay the capital repayments on the mortgage or loan, or the insurance premiums for an endowment mortgage. See Chapter Two for how to negotiate for interest only payments with your lender. Page 51 also suggests ways of trying to pay the unmet part of your mortgage.

- ☐ **Ground rent** if you have a long lease of more than 21 years.
- ☐ **Service charges,** for example, for the maintenance, insurance, management and cleaning of common areas.

In some circumstances, if you are liable to pay housing costs on two homes at the same time, it may be possible to have both amounts included in your income support. This could be if you have left your old home because of fear of domestic violence, or because you are moving house and are liable to pay on both homes for a short period, or if your partner is a student or on a government training course, and has to live away from home. You may need to get advice about this from one of the organisations listed in Appendix 10.

Special note for separated partners: Even if the mortgage is in your partner's name or in joint names, you can still have mortgage interest included as part of your housing requirements if you have to pay the charges in order to keep your home, and the adjudication officer thinks it reasonable to treat you as responsible for the housing costs. Separated partners can also include as part of their housing requirements the interest on any mortgage or loan raised against the house (for example to buy a car), provided the second mortgage or loan was acquired by the other partner either solely or jointly, and the other partner now cannot or will not pay.

Example:
This example shows how the applicable amount is calculated.

Mrs Francis is a single parent with 3 children of 12, 10 and 6. Her mortgage interest payments are £1,906 per year. She has been on benefit for 6 months. Her applicable amount based on April 1988 rates is:

personal allowances		£ p
	for herself	33.40
	for her children	
	6-year-old	10.75
	10-year-old	10.75
	12-yearold	16.10

		£ p
premiums		
	family	6.15
	lone parent	3.70
housing costs		
	mortgage interest	36.65
	(1/52 of yearly figure)	117.50

£117.50 is the level of Mrs Francis' needs. If her income is less than this figure, the difference will be made up by income support.

Your income

Your income consists of the money you have coming into the household each week and any assumed income from your savings. The DHSS will not necessarily take all your income into account in full. The main rules are set out below:

- ☐ **Benefits** such as child benefit or invalidity benefit nearly always count in full as part of your income. The main exceptions are attendance allowance (paid to a disabled person in need of being looked after) and mobility allowance (paid to someone unable or virtually unable to walk). These two benefits are ignored completely.

- ☐ **Maintenance payments** for yourself and your children count in full as part of your income. No distinction is made between maintenance orders paid 'to' or 'for' a child; it all counts. A lump-sum payment of maintenance can lead to you losing your benefit completely for a time, or if the lump sum is for a child, to your benefit being reduced for a time. If your partner pays money to a 'third party' on your behalf (eg, pays your mortgage capital payments to the building society, or some other item that benefit is not intended to cover), then this may be ignored by the DHSS if it would be reasonable to do so. The advice agencies mentioned in Appendix 10 should be able to give you advice about this.

- ☐ **Earnings** from part-time work are not counted in full. First, the adjudication officer will ignore any tax, national insurance, and half of any superannuation that you pay. Then s/he will also ignore the first:

— £15 for people getting the lone parent or disability premiums (and in some cases the higher pensioner premium as well);
or
— £15 from a couple who have been on income support or supplementary benefit for 2 years, and haven't been in full-time work or full-time education during that period;
or
— £5 from the earnings of anyone else.

If your children have any earnings—eg, from a paper round—these are ignored.

☐ Income from a **mortgage insurance policy** will be ignored if it is used to pay any part of your mortgage or loan that is not met by the DHSS (eg, the capital repayments, or where the DHSS is only meeting 50 per cent of your interest payments. See page 47.)

☐ **Tenants** If you let a room and do not provide meals, you will be treated by the local office as having a tenant, even if the terms of your mortgage forbid you to let. Any rent you receive from the tenant is taken into account, apart from the first £4.00. An extra £6.70 is ignored if the rent they pay you includes heating.

☐ **Income from savings** is ignored, provided you have less than £6,000 in savings. However, if you save the income from your savings, it will eventually be counted as part of your savings.

☐ **Savings** and other capital are ignored completely up to £3,000. Above this level, until they reach £6,000, your savings are assumed to give you an income of £1 for each £250 (or part of £250) that you have over £3,000. This is known as **tariff income**. However, some capital or assets which would take your savings over £6,000 are ignored. For example, the surrender value of a life insurance policy is completely ignored. See Appendix 6 for more details on what capital is ignored.

Special note for separated partners: If your home has been sold and you have money as a result of the sale, the local DHSS office will ignore it completely if you intend to use the money to buy another home within 6 months. If you need longer to buy somewhere, the adjudication officer can continue to ignore the money if it is reasonable to do so.

Example

This example shows how income and income support are calculated (based on April 1988 rates).

Ms Francis, a single parent, gets child benefit for her three children (£21.75 per week) plus one parent benefit (£4.90 per week). She has maintenance of £18 per week and works part-time, with net earnings of £20 per week. She has savings of £3,500.

Her income will be assessed as follows:

Child benefit counts in full	£21.75
One parent benefit counts in full	£4.90
Maintenance counts in full	£18.00
£15 of net earnings are ignored for a single parent	£5.00
Tariff income from savings over £3,000 count in full	£2.00
Total income	**£51.65**

Once you know your applicable amount and your income, you can work out how much income support you are entitled to. In the case of Ms Francis, this is:

Her applicable amount (see page 44)	£117.50
Less her income (see above)	£51.65
Her income support is	£65.85

Ms Francis will also receive help with her general rates. Part of these will be paid for her by the local authority (see page 55).

People who were getting supplementary benefit before 11 April 1988

If you were getting supplementary benefit immediately before income support was introduced on 11 April, then you may be receiving an extra payment on top of your income support, (or on top of any other income you have if you are not getting income support). This is called a **transitional addition**, and counts as a payment of income support. It is paid to people whose income under the old supplementary benefit scheme was higher than the amount they would get under the new income support system. You continue to receive this addition as long as your circumstances stay the same, or until income support rates increase to bring your benefit level up to where it was under supplementary benefit.

The rules about when you lose all or some of this addition are very complicated. You may need to get advice if your circumstances change (eg, you have another child). See Appendix 10.

INCOME SUPPORT AND YOUR MORTGAGE INTEREST: WHY YOU MAY GET LESS THAN THE FULL AMOUNT

In most cases, your mortgage interest will be included in full as part of your housing costs. However, in some cases you will not get the full amount.

The first four months on benefit

You will usually only get the full amount of your mortgage or loan interest included in your income support for the first 16 weeks of your claim if you, or your partner, are aged 60 or more. If you, and your partner, are under 60 the DHSS will only pay 50 per cent of your interest payments for the first 16 weeks. After that, they will pay the full amount. This rule will not affect you if:

- ☐ You were getting income support before, and you have only interrupted your claim by less than 8 weeks (eg, you might have taken a temporary job);
- ☐ You have just started claiming as a couple, and your new partner was getting income support less than 8 weeks ago;
- ☐ You have just separated from your partner, and s/he was claiming income support for you less than 8 weeks ago.

In any of these circumstances, the period during which you or your partner were previously getting income support will count towards the 16 weeks.

If you are affected by this rule and you spend more than 16

weeks on benefit you may qualify for additional benefit to meet the interest due on the arrears which will have built up during the time that the DHSS were only meeting 50 per cent of your interest payments.

As a result of this rule you may claim and not qualify for income support where you would have done so if mortgage interest payments had counted in full as part of your applicable amount. In these circumstances, see page 57 for what to do for the first 16 weeks. After 16 weeks promptly make a second claim for income support and your applicable amount should then include your mortgage interest in full.

Your ex-partner's share

If your ex-partner is paying the mortgage, any mortgage capital payments your ex-partner makes to you count as maintenance and will reduce your benefit. However, if your ex-partner pays the capital directly to the lender, the adjudication officer has the discretion to ignore it. If your ex-partner is paying the interest, you will not receive any benefit for the mortgage.

If your ex-partner is not paying the mortgage, you can have the whole of the interest included in your housing requirements, even if you are not legally liable to pay it. Problems can arise where you thought your ex-partner was paying the mortgage and it turns out s/he hasn't been. For help in these circumstances see Appendix 7.

Other people sharing your home (non-dependants)

A 'non-dependant' is someone who lives with you but is not your partner or dependent child and who either pays no rent—eg, a child of yours who has left school but still lives at home, or pays rent which includes a substantial amount for board—eg, a lodger. Non-dependants are expected to contribute towards your housing costs. The amount of contribution or whether any is expected at all is dependent on age and whether or not the person is in work.

The adjudication officer will therefore make the following deductions from the amount you would otherwise get for your housing costs, and ignore any income that you actually receive from the non-dependant. See page 49 for rules about lodgers.

(i) For a non-dependant who is under 18, on a YTS course; a full-time student (except during the summer vacation); under 25 and on income support; or who normally lives elsewhere **no deduction**

(ii) For a non-dependant over 18 in full-time work **£8.20**

(iii) For a lodger paying for board and lodging **£8.20**

(iv) For a non-dependant in full-time work, but with a gross income of less than £49.20 **£3.45**

(v) For a non-dependant over 18 not in full-time work **£3.45**

A deduction will also be made from your rate rebate (see page 55). No deduction at all is made if you or your partner are blind, or getting attendance allowance.

Also, only one deduction will be made where you have a family or couple living with you. The highest appropriate deduction will be made.

Lodgers

A lodger is treated in the same way as a non-dependant (see section above). A fixed deduction is made from your housing costs, and the actual income paid to you by the lodger is ignored up to £35. Above this, any income is taken into account. The DHSS defines a lodger as a person whose payment includes an amount for meals. The arrangement must be on a commercial basis. Someone to whom you rent a room, but for whom you do not provide meals, will probably be treated as your tenant, rather than as a lodger. There is no deduction from your housing costs for a tenant (but see page 45 for how the rent they pay you is treated).

'Excessive' interest payments

The DHSS can refuse to pay the whole of your mortgage interest if they think it is too much. However, this happens very rarely. The Department can only do this if it thinks *either* your home (excluding any rooms you let or which are occupied by lodgers) is unnecessarily large for you and your family, *or* the area in which you live is unnecessarily expensive *or* the cost of the mortgage or the amount of interest is unreasonably high when compared with the costs of suitable alternative accommodation in the area. But if you can show it is not reasonable to expect you to move, the adjudication officer must approve payment of your mortgage interest in full. This can be done by proving that:

- ☐ there is no other suitable accommodation available to you; *or*
- ☐ there is very little cheaper accommodation in the area; *or*
- ☐ your personal circumstances—especially your age, state of health, employment prospects, and the effect of a change of schools on your children—would make it unreasonable to expect you to move.

You can appeal (see page 55) if, contrary to your opinion, the adjudication officer thinks it is reasonable to expect you to move.

In all cases of excessive interest, the adjudication officer must count the whole of your mortgage interest as part of your housing costs for 6 months if you or your partner could afford the mortgage when it was taken on. The interest may continue to be paid in full for a further 6 months after that, if you are doing your best to find cheaper accommodation.

The rules which allow the DHSS to reduce the amount of benefit which you receive towards the mortgage interest apply even if you are already having only 50 per cent of your interest payments met (see page 47). So if you are under 60 and your payments are treated as 'excessive' you get the whole 50 per cent of the mortgage interest paid for your first 16 weeks on benefit, then 100 per cent for 10 weeks and then (because 6 months have passed) you will only receive the restricted amount the DHSS considers reasonable.

Home used for business or other purposes

If a substantial proportion of your house is used for purposes other than as a home for your family—eg, for letting or taking in boarders—in rare circumstances the local authority may decide to count your home as a 'mixed hereditament' and not just a private dwelling. If this happens, you should probably get advice from one of the organisations mentioned in Appendix 10 and appeal against the decision. Your house may also be classed as a mixed hereditament where part of your house includes an empty shop which you also own.

You will only be entitled to help with that proportion of the mortgage interest which is equal to the proportion of the rateable value for the part of the house you actually live in. For example, if you have an empty shop which takes up 80 per cent of the total valuation of your property, the DHSS will pay only 20 per cent of the total mortgage interest.

During the first 16 weeks on income support you will be entitled to only 50 per cent of the total mortgage interest that would normally be paid (see page 47). In the above example, the person would get a mere 10 per cent paid for the first 16 weeks.

If your house is classed as a 'mixed hereditament' and, as a result, you get very limited help with your mortgage interest payments, you should get advice from a local advice agency (see Appendix 10 at the end of this Guide).

You have bought the house or flat you previously rented

If, whilst receiving income support, you buy the flat or house you used to rent *and* you previously had security of tenure (for example your landlord did not live on the premises or you were a council tenant), the DHSS will not necessarily pay for any increase in your housing costs. Instead, they will limit your income support 'housing costs' to the amount of rent used to calculate your housing benefit when you were a tenant. If, subsequently, your housing costs rise again, you will be allowed to include the second rise as part of your housing requirements. This restriction can only be lifted if there is a 'major change' in your family's circumstances which makes it difficult for you to pay your housing costs—eg, you bought the house jointly with your working son who has now moved out or who has become unemployed.

HOW TO PAY THE UNMET INTEREST, MORTGAGE CAPITAL OR INSURANCE PREMIUMS

These are some suggestions for how you can try to meet any part of your housing costs not being paid by the DHSS. However, if the problem is that your lender is refusing to accept interest only payments, it is worth negotiating on this point, before trying to raise the cash. See Chapter Two for suggestions on how to negotiate.

Get a part-time job

A small amount of your earnings will be ignored by the local DHSS office when they work out your benefit (see page 45). So you could put this money towards the unmet part of your mortgage.

Childminding

There are special rules for someone who is on benefit and working as a childminder. This is because the DHSS will ignore two-thirds of the money s/he makes and only count a third as earnings.

Example:
Sue is a single parent and has a three-year-old child. She minds two other toddlers. She charges £21 for each child per week. Out of the £42 Sue receives, the DHSS will ignore two-thirds (£28) and treat only one-third (£14) as earnings.

As a single parent she is allowed to keep the first £15 of her earnings. Since the DHSS is treating her as having earnings of only £14, all of her earnings as a childminder will be ignored. So she will keep the whole £42, although she will, of course, have to spend some of it on food, paint, toys, etc, for the children she is minding.

Take in a lodger

You will be allowed to keep any money you receive from a lodger up to £35. There will be a fixed deduction from the income support you get for your housing costs of £8.20, and your rate rebate will also be reduced (see page 56). This leaves you with up to £26.80 which is disregarded, which will have to cover your costs (such as food and fuel), as well as any profit. It may be worth working out roughly how much you would have to spend on providing board and lodging, so you know whether it will be worth your while having a lodger.

But there are some difficulties to watch out for if you take in a lodger who receives income support.

First, if s/he is under 26 and on income support, there are

restrictions on the length of time for which the DHSS will pay their lodgings charge in any 6-month period, unless they do not have to sign on as a condition of receiving benefit or are exempt from this rule; consult CPAG's *National Welfare Benefits Handbook* or one of the organisations listed in Appendix 10 for more information.

Second, irrespective of age, there are maximum amounts which DHSS will pay to a lodger on income support, which are supposed to cover not only the board and lodging charge but also meals taken outside of the accommodation. The limits range from £45-£70 per week depending upon where you live, and £1.55 of this is to cover each lunch or evening meal taken outside the lodgings, £1.10 for every breakfast so taken. Again you should enquire further about this if it affects your lodger.

A special note if you take a tenant or a lodger

- ☐ *Your social security office:* You have to let your office know of any changes in your circumstances. You should write to the DHSS explaining what new arrangements you have made and if you want them to treat the new person as a lodger, it is important that you say that you are providing cooked meals. It is vital that you do this if you are a single parent and offer a room to someone of the opposite sex. A written statement from you at the office should prevent any problems over neighbours or others telling the office that you and your lodger are 'cohabiting'. You could risk losing your benefit (see page 38). Keep a copy of your letter.
- ☐ *Your lender:* Your mortgage agreement will probably state that you must not let a room or take in a lodger. If you have already let a room and there are no problems with the mortgage, the chances are that your lender will not bother about what you are doing. However, if you are trying to negotiate a change in your mortgage with your lender and they discover that you are letting a room, they may be unwilling to help you. It would be safer from this point of view to look at some of the other ways of raising extra cash (see above).
- ☐ *Your lodger/tenant:* Don't forget that you are offering someone a home even if it is in your own house. Depending on the arrangements between you they could have some limited rights in that home under the Rent Acts or other laws which deal with landlords and tenants. In particular you might be responsible

for minor repairs or find it difficult to make them leave immediately if things don't work out. Ask for advice on this from one of the agencies listed in Appendix 10 *before* you take anyone in.

Help from a friend, relative or charity

If you have a friend, relative or charity who is prepared to pay the unmet mortgage interest or mortgage capital or insurance premiums for you, this amount will not reduce your weekly benefit. However, the friend or relative must not be your ex-husband, or the father of your children. Any money from him counts in full as maintenance unless he pays the money direct to the lender, when the DHSS has discretion to ignore this (see page 44). The money from the friend or relative will be ignored by the adjudication officer because it is paying for something which your income support is not meant to cover.

Benefit arrears

Another way to raise money to pay your housing costs, and other bills, is to check whether or not you are owed arrears of income support. If you are, these will be paid as a cash lump sum. First, check your current weekly benefit for all the different elements described on pages 41-43. You may not be getting them all or the amount you are receiving may be wrong (check the figures in Appendix 5). There might even have been a simple mathematical error made in adding them up. If you find something is wrong or missing, write in and ask that it be put right and your arrears paid. If it was the DHSS office that made a mistake, the arrears can be backdated indefinitely. If you are getting less because you failed to report something, your arrears can only be backdated for a maximum of one year. If you were on supplementary benefit before April 1988, you may have been underpaid then. An advice centre may be able to check this for you. The second way to get arrears is to ask for your whole claim for income support to be backdated. You can do this where you find that you could have qualified for benefit before the date on which you actually claimed and you had a good reason for not claiming earlier (see page 39).

CHALLENGING DECISIONS ABOUT YOUR INCOME SUPPORT

If the local DHSS office refuses to give you what you ask for, it is always worth considering whether to appeal. You can get help in deciding whether to appeal or not from the organisations listed in Appendix 10.

You appeal simply by writing to the adjudication officer at your local DHSS office and saying that you wish to appeal against the decision. It is usually best to give a full explanation of why you disagree with the decision. In some cases, this may lead to the decision being changed without you having to go to the tribunal. You have 3 months from the date of the adjudication officer's decision in which to appeal.

About 5-6 weeks later, the clerk to the tribunal will send you a note of the date, time and place of the hearing. You will also receive the appeal papers, which include an explanation of how your benefit has been calculated, a copy of your appeal letter and a statement from the adjudication officer explaining the reasons for his/her decision. You should get these about a week before the hearing. It is crucial that you go to the hearing yourself and that, if possible, you get help in preparing and presenting your case. If you can't attend the tribunal for whatever reason, or need more time to prepare your case, write to the clerk to the tribunal and ask for an adjournment.

OTHER RELATED BENEFITS

Rate rebate

Your entitlement to income support means that you will almost certainly qualify for a rate rebate. There is a claim form for this tucked inside the income support claim for which can be returned to the DHSS, or the local authority. You can also apply directly to the local authority on its own application form.

You are entitled to a rebate in the following circumstances:

- if you are legally liable to pay the rates;
- if you actually pay them and are either the partner of the person who is liable, or the local authority thinks it reasonable to treat you as entitled to a rebate.

A rate rebate is part of what is called housing benefit, and is paid by the local authority in the form of a reduced or nil rates demand.

The calculation of a rebate for people on income support is much simpler than for other people. If you receive income support, your income is automatically considered low enough to get the maximum level of rate rebate, and in most cases this will be 80 per cent of your general rates. Everyone now has to pay, out of their other income, at least 20 per cent of the rates. However, in any of the following situations you may get less than 80 per cent:

- □ **If you have a non-dependant living with you**, your rebate will be reduced by £3.00 per week (see page 48 for an explanation of non-dependant). You will therefore have to pay this additional amount towards the rates yourself, or collect it from the non-dependant. No deduction will be made from your rate rebate, however, if, *either*:
  - — you or your partner are blind, or receiving attendance allowance; *or*
  - — the non-dependant is 16 or 17, normally lives elsewhere, is on a YTS course and isn't a commercial lodger, or is a full-time student (except during the summer holidays), or normally lives somewhere else.

- □ **Your rates are considered excessive**. If the local authority considers that your rates are unreasonably high compared to other suitable homes, or that your home is unreasonably large for your needs, they can base your rebate on a lower figure. However, this power should not be used very often, and in many cases should only be used if it would be reasonable to expect you to move. If the local authority reduces your rebate in this way, get advice from one of the organisations in Appendix 10.

The local authority must notify you of how much your rate rebate is. You can also write and ask for a more detailed explanation of how the rebate has been calculated. If you are unhappy about the amount of your rebate, you have a right to ask the local authority to review its decision within 6 weeks of being notified of it. If still dissatisfied, you have 28 days to ask for a further review by a review board. You can get further advice on how to challenge a local authority's decision concerning your rate rebate from the organisations listed in Appendix 10. See page 28 for how to get more housing benefit in exceptional circumstances. For other ways of reducing your rates, see page 28.

Help with your community charge (poll tax)

In April 1989 in Scotland, rates are being replaced by the community charge (or 'poll tax' as it is more commonly known). A rebate scheme is due to be introduced which will probably be very similar to the present rate rebate system. For more details, from April 1989, readers in Scotland should contact their local authority, or one of the agencies listed in Appendix 10.

Health and education benefits

Income support gives automatic entitlement to a range of health and education benefits. You and your family will be entitled to:

- ☐ free prescriptions;
- ☐ free dental treatment;
- ☐ optical vouchers;
- ☐ milk tokens and free vitamins for expectant and nursing mothers and children under school age;
- ☐ refunds of hospital fares for treatment;
- ☐ free school meals.

THE SOCIAL FUND

The social fund replaces the old single payment grants that were available as part of the supplementary benefit scheme. Unlike the single payments system, most payments from the social fund are discretionary—normally you do not have a right to receive a payment (the only exceptions are payments for funerals, maternity needs, and cold weather). The fund has a limited budget, so if it runs out during the year, no more payments can be made. If you are refused a payment from the social fund, there is no independent right of appeal, although you can ask for an internal 'review' of the decision. Social fund officers work from local social security offices.

Most payments made by the social fund will be loans that have to be repaid out of weekly benefit. Some grants will be made, however, and these are called **community care grants**.

Community Care Grants (CCG)

You generally have to be on income support to apply for a CCG, and the law says that you can get one in order to:

- ☐ help you re-establish yourself in the community after a period in institutional or residential care;

  or

- ☐ enable you to remain living in the community, rather than going into institutional or residential care;

  or

- ☐ help ease exceptional pressures on you or your family;

  or

- ☐ help with certain travel expenses.

Since all decisions are at the discretion of the social fund officer, there are few rules about when you should get a community care grant, and for what. The rules do say, however, that when deciding whether to make a payment, the social fund officer should take account of any other resources that you have available to meet the need. If they do decide to make a payment, the amount will be reduced if you have any savings over £500.

The following are some examples of when the DHSS suggest people may receive community care grants:

- ☐ start-up grants for people setting up home for the first time;
- ☐ removals grants in a variety of situations;
- ☐ fares for people moving house;
- ☐ furniture and furnishings for people moving from unfurnished accommodation, or when essential furniture has been damaged;
- ☐ grants for minor structural repairs and maintenance costs, where the work is essential to keep the home habitable;
- ☐ connection or re-connection fees;
- ☐ grants for decoration and refurbishment for some groups of people;
- ☐ clothing grants where, for example, you are unable to recover your clothes from your former home because of domestic violence.

However, they are only examples. If you consider that you have a need, which fits one of the four general situations listed at the beginning of this section then go ahead and apply.

Loans

The social fund also make **budgeting loans** to people who have been on income support for 6 months. These are intended to cover a variety of different one-off needs that are difficult to budget for out of weekly benefit. These loans may be available for a wide range of things, including furniture, minor house repairs, removal charges, redecoration, etc. There are also crisis loans for meeting needs in an emergency, or after a disaster (eg, like a fire, or flood). You do not necessarily have to be on income support to get a crisis loan. Emergencies might include loss of money, or when you are waiting for your first benefit payment after your initial claim.

Although these loans are interest-free, they are recovered by deductions from weekly benefit at what is often a very high weekly rate. They can also be recovered from your partner's benefit. You should think very carefully about whether you can manage to live on what may be a very reduced level of benefit, before accepting a social fund loan.

BENEFITS TO CLAIM IF YOU ARE NOT ENTITLED TO INCOME SUPPORT

Even if you do not qualify for income support, there may be other benefits you are entitled to. Many of them are listed in Chapter Three.

- ☐ a rate rebate (page 25);
- ☐ child benefit and one parent benefit (pages 30-31);
- ☐ education benefits (pages 31-32);
- ☐ health benefits (page 32);
- ☐ certain tax allowances (page 33).

CHAPTER FIVE

Repairs and improvements

The need for repairs to your home can be a serious worry when you are trying to make ends meet on a tight budget. Similarly, there may be improvements you wish to make to your home which would make life a lot easier, if only you could afford them. In this chapter we outline the various ways you can try to raise the money to pay for the necessary work.

LOANS OR GRANTS FOR REPAIRS AND IMPROVEMENTS FROM THE DHSS

Budgeting loans

It may be possible to get a loan from the social fund to meet the cost of some repairs and improvements. The guidance lists the following as high priority items for a budgeting loan:

- any application where refusal could cause either hardship, damage or risk to the health or safety of you or/and your family;
- essential home repairs and maintenance for owner occupiers if a bank loan/mortgage is not available.

To get a budgeting loan you must:

- be in receipt of income support at the date of the award of the loan; *and*
- have been in receipt of income support, or the partner of someone in receipt of income support, either for each week of the last 26 weeks, less a single period of not less than 14 days.

If you have been in receipt of supplementary benefit, this will count towards the 26-week period.

You cannot get a budgeting loan if you or your partner is involved in a trade dispute.

If the social fund officer decides to make a payment, s/he will reduce the amount you receive by the amount of savings you have over £500.

How to apply for a budgeting loan

Applications for budgeting loans have to be made in writing by the applicant or by someone acting on his/her behalf, on an approved form, delivered to any local office of DHSS. However, social fund officers are told to accept a letter if it contains enough information for them to make a decision.

Community care grants

You must be receiving income support on the day that you apply for a community care grant, or if you are about to be discharged from an institution you must be within 6 weeks of discharge and likely to receive income support on discharge.

In some circumstances it may be possible to get a community care grant to carry out repairs and improvements. These grants are meant to 'promote community care', and are directed at 'priority groups'. The priority groups are:

- ☐ elderly people, particularly those with restricted mobility or those who have difficulty performing personal tasks;
- ☐ mentally handicapped people;
- ☐ mentally ill people;
- ☐ physically disabled people, including people who are sensorily impaired;
- ☐ chronically sick people, especially terminally ill people;
- ☐ people who have misused alcohol or drugs;
- ☐ ex-offenders requiring resettlement;
- ☐ people without a settled way of life undergoing resettlement;
- ☐ families under stress;
- ☐ young people leaving care of the local authority.

The guidance says that promoting community care means helping people, especially those in vulnerable groups, to return to live in the community or remain living in the community.

Any capital you or your partner have in excess of £500 is treated in the same way as for a budgeting loan. If you or your partner are involved in a trade dispute you cannot get a community care grant except for travelling expenses in certain situations. The guidance sets out two circumstances in which a community care grant may be payable for repairs and improvements.

(i) Awards for people in vulnerable groups who are staying in the community rather than entering institutional or residential care and who are improving their living conditions

Awards for minor structural repairs and maintenance costs

A maximum amount of £400 is suggested for this and the guidance says a grant can only be made where:

- ☐ You are responsible for the repairs; *and*
- ☐ The home does not belong to a local authority or a similar body, eg, housing association; *and*
- ☐ The local authority does not have a duty to carry out the work under the Chronically Sick and Disabled Persons Act; *and*
- ☐ There are no other readily available means to meet the cost (eg, help from a local authority, relatives or charities).

Social fund officers are told to satisfy themselves that unless the work is done on the home, you are likely to be taken into institutional or residential care. They are also told to ask you for an estimate of the work.

If you need to have major structural repairs or improvements done such as stabilising foundations, replacing floors or staircases for example, the interest on a mortgage or loan to pay for this may be available from income support.

A community care grant can be made to cover any necessary survey fees but not the legal fees involved in arranging a loan.

(ii) Awards to ease exceptional pressure on families

Exceptional pressure as defined in the guidance can be because of 'a deterioration in your home which makes it unfit or unsuitable for you or your family to live there'.

Minor structural repairs to keep the home habitable, or safe for a child

Priority is to be given to applications from families with a disabled child.

If your home is structurally unsafe or unsanitary, and only major repairs will solve the problem, you may be awarded removal expenses as an alternative to a grant for minor structural repairs. Otherwise the guidance says awards should not normally be made in these circumstances.

The maximum suggested grant is £400, and the conditions are the same as for (i) above, except that the rule saying that you or your partner are likely to be taken into institutional or residential care unless the work is done, does not apply.

How to apply for a community care grant

The rule for making applications is the same as for budgeting loans. If you are not considered to be eligible for a community care grant, social fund officers are told to treat your application as an application for a budgeting loan and then for a crisis loan if you appear to be in 'considerable need' and there is a serious risk to your or your family's health or/and safety.

For a full explanation of the discretionary social fund and the reviews and complaints procedures, see CPAG's *National Welfare Benefits Handbook* or *Guide to the Social Fund Manual*, both available from CPAG Ltd, 1-5 Bath St, London EC1. If you need advice on your application to the social fund, contact one of the agencies listed in Appendix 10.

GRANTS FROM THE LOCAL AUTHORITY

There are a number of grants you can get from your local authority to help with repairs and improvements.

Improvement grants

You can get these to finance improvements in your home such as putting in a damp proof course, extending a bathroom which is too small, or installing a modern electrical circuit. Improvement grants can also include money for helping towards repairs and/or be used to finance the conversion of larger houses into flats.

Repair grants

You can only get this if your home was built before 1919, and the repairs required are 'substantial and structural'—eg, a new roof or underpinning foundations.

Intermediate grants (or Scotland standard amenities grants)

These grants are given to enable you to put in one or more standard amenities if you do not already have them. Standard amenities include items such as a bath, shower, washbasin, sink, wc and hot and cold water supplies to all of these. Unlike improvement grants and most repair grants the local authority must give you an intermediate grant if you meet some basic conditions.

Special grants

These are available to landlords for installing the same standard amenities as for intermediate grants and to pay for fire escape areas.

Common parts grants

This is a new type of grant for improvement or repairs to the common parts of buildings that are divided into flats, eg, the roof or common staircase. Either the owner of the building or the tenant/leaseholder of an individual flat can apply for the grants.

Insulation grants

These are given for insulating lofts, lagging pipes and hot water tanks.

How to get a grant from the local authority

You must first apply to your local authority grants section. This may be part of the housing department or possibly the environmental health department. Check with the town hall. If the local authority think you qualify for a grant you will have to fill in an application form and someone from the local authority will come to inspect your home (occasionally the local authority may inspect first if there is any doubt about the work required). After the inspection, the local authority will let you know what work is required and, if there are to be major alterations, they may ask you to have plans drawn up. You will have to pay for these yourself *before* you know whether or not you are eligible for a grant. If you are successful in getting a local authority grant, you can claim back the amount you spent on fees for plans, etc, as part of your costs.

The purpose of giving a grant is to help people put their homes into good repair. The local authority, therefore, may ask for a lot more work to be done than you had planned. In some circumstances you may *have* to do some extra work to get your grant, but in other cases the local authority have the discretion to accept more limited standards of improvement. They may use this discretion if, for example, there is an elderly or ill person in the house who would find the upheaval too much or if you could not raise enough money to finance the full works asked for. Discuss this with your local authority.

Once you and the local authority have agreed the work to be done, you will have to get estimates of the cost of the work, and submit them to the local authority. Some local authorities provide a list of local builders you can use, otherwise you will have to find one yourself. Once all this has been done, the local authority will decide whether or not to approve your grant. *You must never start work before you have had official approval or you could lose any chance of a grant.*

If you fulfil the qualifying conditions, you have a *right* to an intermediate grant but, generally speaking, the other grants are at the discretion of the local authority.

If you are refused a grant you could try appealing to a local councillor to see if the local authority will change their mind.

Sometimes local authorities run out of money to give grants so, if you can, it is best to get your application in near the beginning of the financial year (April). If you are refused a grant because there is no money left, apply again in the new financial year.

The grant will not cover the full cost of the work but a percentage ranging between 50 per cent and 90 per cent. If you live in a special area such as a Housing Action Area or General Improvement Area, the percentage of the grant will be higher. Anyone who is considered to be in financial hardship (see below) may get 90 per cent if their local authority agree. At different times the government also sets more generous limits for the scheme, so it is always worth checking if a higher percentage is available. *Home Improvement Grants*, published by the Department of the Environment, sets out the basic details of the different schemes available (see Appendix 11).

You may qualify for a higher grant if your local authority decides that you could not pay your share of the work without undue hardship. In assessing 'hardship', many local authorities simply look at your income (and possibly savings) in relation to your outgoings. If your income is income support, you may qualify automatically. They may also take into account your ability to raise a loan. If you are refused a loan as large as you need, you can ask the local authority to reconsider the percentage of grant you are being offered.

LOANS FROM OTHER SOURCES

If you don't succeed in getting a grant for repairs and improvements from the local authority, you may be able to get a loan from other sources—eg, a bank, building society, or a reputable finance company, to pay for the work. Even if you do qualify for a local authority grant, it is likely you will still have to raise a loan for the part of the work not met by the amount awarded.

Loans taken out before 6 April 1988 for the purposes of home improvements will be eligible for tax relief. Loans taken out for repairs, or any loans taken out after 6 April 1988 are no longer eligible for tax relief.

Note: If you need to raise additional finance to pay for repairs and improvements and this is added to your existing loan, the whole loan will be taken out of the MIRAS system, and tax relief on the original part of your loan will have to be claimed directly from the Inland Revenue.

Borrowers who are not required to pay tax (eg, who are in receipt of benefits), would then not be eligible to claim tax relief on mortgage payments.

However, if the money you need to raise is treated as a separate loan, the original loan will remain eligible for tax relief under the MIRAS system.

How much will a loan cost?

Raising an extra loan on top of your mortgage will not necessarily cost you much more each month. For example, if you had a £20,000 loan over 25 years, and were paying interest on it at 11.5 per cent, the monthly net repayment would be £164.40. An extra £3,000 you borrowed to meet repairs spread out over the same period of time would cost you an additional £30.78 per month without tax relief. Appendix 2 shows you how to work out how much *your* loan would cost.

How will you pay for a loan?

If you are receiving income support

The DHSS will increase your benefit to cover some or all of the interest payable on any loan you manage to get for major repairs necessary to maintain the fabric of your home or for the following improvements:

- ☐ putting in bathroom fixtures, eg, washbasin, bath, shower or toilet;
- ☐ damp proofing;
- ☐ providing or improving ventilation or natural light;
- ☐ providing or improving drainage facilities;
- ☐ putting in electric lighting and sockets;
- ☐ putting in heating, including central heating;
- ☐ putting in storage facilities for fuel and refuse;
- ☐ improving the structural condition of the home;
- ☐ improving facilities for storing, preparing and cooking food;
- ☐ insulation;
- ☐ other improvements which are reasonable in the circumstances.

The DHSS may assist with survey fees you have to pay while trying to arrange the loan through the social fund community care grants or budgeting loans. If you have savings of more than £500, the DHSS will expect you to put what excess you have over £500 towards the cost of the work, and will only pay you the interest on the balance.

If you are only receiving 50 per cent of your mortgage interest from the DHSS for the first 16 weeks of your claim (see page 47) you will similarly only qualify for 50 per cent help with the interest on any loan for repairs or improvements. If you are still on benefit after 16 weeks you will then start to get 100 per cent of the interest on the loan and a payment to meet the interest which will have accumulated on the 50 per cent interest unpaid during the first 16 weeks.

If you are not receiving income support

You will need to make sure that your income is enough to meet the increased payments. See Chapter Three and Chapter Four for ways of maximising your income. You will also want to make sure that your loan is arranged on the cheapest possible basis; see Chapter Two for advice on this. Your lender will calculate how much you are able to borrow on the basis of your total income.

How to get a loan

You should approach your present lender first. If you have an expensive endowment mortgage or a loan from a finance company, you may wish to rearrange all your loans on a cheaper basis with a building society, bank or local authority. See Chapter Two for more information on this.

Your lender will look at the work required and its costs, your income and your property. Normally the property will be valued (you will have to pay for this) before your lender decides whether to give you a loan. There will be some legal and administrative fees involved in granting a second loan, so check with your lender how much these will be. You can try asking your lender to include the fees as part of the loan.

If you are refused a loan by your present lender, you will have to look for alternative sources of money (the obvious first alternative being a bank). Wherever you are borrowing the additional money from, check the details of the loan very carefully. Some short-term bank loans (up to 5 years) are charged at quite a high interest rate, so are to be avoided. It is always the case that the shorter the repayment period the higher the monthly cost, so always try to get your loan over the longest possible term, 20-25 years if you can.

Negotiating with your lender

First you will have to find out how much you need to borrow. Then you will have to show your lender how you will meet the payments. Write to your lender giving details of:

- ☐ estimates of the cost of the work (send a copy of your original);
- ☐ any grant you will be getting from your local authority (or say that you are applying and will send further information later);
- ☐ how much you are likely to need to borrow.

Then you will need to show how you will meet the payments.

If you are receiving income support

- ☐ Send a letter from your DHSS office confirming that they are prepared in principle to meet the interest on the additional payments whether in whole or in part.
- ☐ Explain *either* the way in which you can meet the capital/insurance premium that the DHSS will not pay (see pages 51-54 for suggestions on how to do this), *or* that you would like the lender to waive the capital part of the mortgage until you are in a position to start paying it. Give some idea how and when this might be.

See Appendix 8 for an example of a letter to send to your lender.

If you are not receiving income support

- ☐ Give details of your income, and what it is comprised of. If your income is likely to increase in the near future, say so. See pages 20 and 37 for ways of increasing your income.
- ☐ Show how you will be able to meet the payments on the loan, as well as your other outgoings. You can do this by listing your outgoings in detail, and showing the money you have left over once those commitments are paid.

See Appendix 8 for an example of a letter to send to your lender.

CHAPTER SIX

Dealing with arrears

If you do not make your monthly payments, your lender can apply to the court for an order giving the lender the right to evict you from your home, so that it can be sold and the proceeds used to pay off the loan.

However, it is never too late for you to take steps to try to keep your home. Even if your position seems hopeless, there are several ways in which you can arrange to clear your arrears. If you can do this and, at the same time, cut your future mortgage costs (see Chapter Two) and increase your income (see Chapter Three and Chapter Four), you will be able to keep your home knowing that you can manage from now on.

This chapter explains the steps your lenders will take to get their money back when you fall behind with your payments. It goes on to explain what you must do to stop the action they are taking and to bring your mortgage(s) back up to date. It also explains what happens if you cannot come to any arrangement with your lenders. If you would like advice, contact one of the organisations listed in Appendix 10.

HOW LENDERS RECLAIM A LOAN

Any lender who has a 'charge' on your home will be able to apply to the County Court for a possession order. Once the order has been made, the lender can take over your home and sell it to get back their money. The stages of your lender's action are as follows:

- ☐ As soon as your mortgage payments stop, **your lender will write** and ask you to make arrangements to bring your payments up to date.

- ☐ If you continue to miss making your mortgage repayments and/or fail to clear your arrears, your lender will write again, **threatening to take legal proceedings**. This means that they are thinking of instructing their solicitors to apply to the court for an order for possession of your home.

- ☐ **Your lender will pass details of your mortgage to their solicitors.** From this time on the solicitors will act on the lender's behalf.

- ☐ **The court will send you a summons**. This is a form which orders you to appear in court and gives the date of the hearing. You will also receive a document headed 'Particulars of Claim' which your lender's solicitor will have drafted, setting out the details of the mortgage agreement and the amount of arrears alleged. Attached is another form which you should fill in and return within 14 days, stating whether or not you agree with the facts your lenders have given and what you are proposing to do about them.

- ☐ **The court hearing will take place**. You will have the chance to state your circumstances and explain the arrangements you are able to make to clear the arrears and keep up the full monthly payments in the future. If you are in a position to pay off all the arrears, there and then, and provide evidence that you will be able to make the full payments in future, the court will probably refuse to make any kind of possession order against you.

  However, even if you cannot pay off all the arrears straightaway, the court has wide powers under Section 36 of the Administration of Justice Act 1970 to adjourn the proceedings or make a **suspended possession order** if it thinks that the borrower is likely to be able to repay the arrears within a reasonable period. You should explain your proposals for clearing the arrears to the court (see page 73).

  A suspended possession order will not entitle your lender to evict you so long as you keep up the payments ordered by the court. If you do not, your lender will be able to apply for a **possession warrant** and have you evicted by the court bailiffs without having to arrange another hearing in court. When a suspended possession order is made you can ask the court to order that a possession warrant should not be issued without a further hearing for the court to give permission. It will be at the court's discretion to agree to this part of the suspended order.

If the court decides your position is a hopeless one, it will make an outright **possession order**, ordering possession within, normally, 28 days.

- ☐ **The lender can apply for a possession warrant** on or after the date specified in the court order; you don't *have* to leave on that date. Once the court office has processed the application, it will give the necessary details to the bailiffs, who will fix a date and time for the eviction. The bailiffs will then write to you giving you the eviction date.
- ☐ If you are still there when the bailiffs arrive, they will evict you from your home and either remove your belongings at the same time or make arrangements with you for their removal.

HOW TO KEEP YOUR HOME

Do not stop paying your mortgage completely just because you cannot afford the whole amount. You should pay what you can whilst you take steps to lower your mortgage costs and increase your income (see Chapters One, Two and Three). You also need to make sure that you will be able to manage in the future. You must take steps to stop your lender's action and see about clearing your arrears.

Stopping your lender's action

You must act quickly, especially if the court or the bailiff is already involved. It is never too late to try to keep your home. What you should do depends on how far your lender's action has gone.

- ☐ **You are under pressure from your lender but they have not yet applied to the court for a hearing** (see page 71). Write back to your lender straightaway. Tell them that you are making every effort to clear your arrears and that you will let them know your proposals on this within, say, one month. Explain how your circumstances have changed and how you hope to make your mortgage payments in future. Ask them to help you cut your mortgage costs in any of the ways appropriate (see page 11). If your lender refuses to negotiate with you and says that the action is going ahead, ask for help from a person in higher authority and send them a copy of your earlier letter. The person to write to would be the General Manager of your building society or finance company, or your local councillor if your loan is from the local authority.

☐ **You have received a court summons** (see page 71). If you have not already been writing to your lender as above, you should try to get the court hearing adjourned to give you time to look at ways of clearing your arrears. Ideally, you want to get your lender's agreement to the adjournment. If the court hearing is more than a week away, write to your lender's solicitor setting out how you are intending to clear the arrears (see page 75) and make future payments. Ask the solicitor to agree to adjourn the hearing to give you the time you need to negotiate. If your lender's solicitors refuse to agree to an adjournment and you believe they are being unreasonable in not agreeing to one, it is worth considering making an application to the court for an adjournment. Your lender's solicitors have to be given at least 2 days' notice of the application.

☐ **The court hearing is to take place** (see page 71). If for some reason, you have not been able to prepare your case and negotiate with your lender before the hearing (perhaps you learned about it too late), you can ask the judge (in some courts, the registrar), to agree to an adjournment. In any event, you must go along to the court on the date of the hearing and be ready to put your case, because the adjournment may not be allowed. It is a good idea to take a friend or adviser with you (see Appendix 10). Remember that the case is all about money. If you are arguing against an outright possession order being granted, you will have to explain how you are going to clear the arrears (see page 75) and pay for your mortgage in future. The judge will be more interested in this than in the reasons for your difficulties.

How to prepare your case

Before you read this section, you should consider getting legal help (see Appendix 9 which gives the background to the Legal Aid Scheme). Your basic task is to show how you can clear your arrears either in a lump sum payment or gradually over a period of months, or by a combination of the two. Tell the court:

- ☐ how much money, if any, you have, or will have, to pay as a lump sum;
- ☐ the steps you are taking to raise a lump sum;
- ☐ how much you are *certain* of being able to pay each month to clear the arrears;
- ☐ the steps you are hoping to take to lower your mortgage costs and/or increase your income so that you can manage in future.

How much should you offer to pay?

Do not over-commit yourself. You must balance the need to clear your debt as soon as possible with the importance of making an offer which you know you will be able to keep up. Do not be put off from making an offer in court because your lender has already told you that it is too low or that the arrears must be cleared more quickly. If you are on income support mention the possibility of direct payments to meet the interest and something towards the arrears (see page 75). It is up to the judge to decide what is reasonable. If you make an offer in court which you are unable to keep, it will be harder (if not impossible) to convince the judge of your good faith when you return to fight a possession application for the second time. On the other hand, the more quickly you can offer to repay the arrears, the better your chances are of staying in your home. If the judge does not accept your case against the possession order, you should ask for enough time to sell your home and find alternative accommodation (see Chapter Eight).

- ☐ **If your lender has been granted a possession order and has perhaps already applied for a possession warrant** (see page 72), you can apply to the court for another hearing if you have any new proposals which you were not able to make at the last hearing. You can do this whatever stage your lender's action has reached as long as you have not yet been actually evicted. The court has power to prevent an eviction even where a possession warrant has been obtained and a date for the eviction set, but you will have to move very fast to get a hearing in time.

  At the same time, write to your lender's solicitors to set out your new proposals. It is vital that you apply for a fresh hearing if you were not able to put your case at the last one. This may have been because you were sick or at work, or did not know about the legal action, for instance, if you are separated and the information was sent to your partner only.

CLEARING YOUR MORTGAGE ARREARS

You can do this by paying a lump sum to your lender or by paying off a little each month over a specific period of time, or by a combination of both. Your first move must be to find out exactly how much you owe to your lender(s) now. Write to each of them and ask for a statement of your account(s).

Special note for separated partners If the mortgage is not in your name, you may find that the lender is unwilling to give you the figures you need. There are other options you can follow:

- ☐ Try and get your partner to give your lender written permission to release the figures to you.
- ☐ Explain to your lender that you wish to make the repayments in future and to clear the arrears. If you are married, stress that you have the right to make payments in your spouse's place under Section 1(5) of the Matrimonial Homes Act 1983. State that you need to know details of the accounts so that you can make payments.

Direct payments

The lender may be prepared to postpone action against you if you are on income support and you offer to have the interest payments and a small amount towards the arrears deducted from your benefit and paid direct to the lender. This gives the lender the reassurance that current payments will be met even if the arrears are only being cleared by a regular token amount. You need to write to the DHSS and ask them to put you on the direct payments scheme. If you are having other debts cleared by direct payments (eg, to the fuel board) there is a maximum total amount deductible and in any event you should only agree to the deduction of an amount towards the arrears if it leaves you enough benefit to live on.

How to raise a lump sum

There are at least five different ways of trying to do this.

Apply to your social security office

- ☐ *If you are already receiving income support* make sure that you are getting the right amount (see Appendix 5), and your appropriate mortgage interest). If for any reason you have not been receiving your full entitlement, write to the local office and ask them to review the amount of benefit they have been paying and to pay any arrears due, back to the date when you claimed benefit. Arrears of income support can be backdated by up to 12 months.

- ☐ *If you are not claiming income support,* check whether you qualify for it (see pages 37-59). If you might qualify, claim at once. The local office has the power to backdate your claim if there is a good reason why your claim was late. For instance, you may have claimed another benefit, like unemployment benefit, thinking this would cover your needs and now find that you were entitled to some income support as well. You may have been wrongly advised by the DHSS, an advice centre or a solicitor that you were not entitled to claim; or there may be other good reasons why you did not claim earlier. Ask the benefit officer to use his/her power to backdate and appeal if you are refused (see page 55).

- ☐ *If you are not entitled to income support,* check whether you can claim family credit. Family credit can also be backdated for up to 12 months if you can show good cause for a late claim.

> **Special note for separated partners** You may get a lump sum payment if you have not been getting any income support or only a reduced amount, because it was thought your partner was paying the mortgage interest and s/he hasn't been. See Appendix 7.

Apply to your local social services department if you have children under 16.

Write, asking them to make you a payment using their power under Section 1 of the Child Care Act 1980 and explain that you and your children are threatened with eviction and homelessness because of your mortgage arrears. Most social services departments do not have much money available and will usually want to know that you have already applied to your social security office if you are now receiving income support.

Change your type of mortgage

If you have a 'with profits' endowment mortgage ask your lender to convert it to the capital repayment basis and to allow you to use the 'surrender value' of your life policy to repay your mortgage arrears (see page 13).

Apply to a charity

The Directory of Grant Making Trusts, which you can find at your local library, has a full list of charities and gives a brief outline of the categories of people they are prepared to consider for grants. It is always worth looking through this book under such headings as the occupations of your family, particular illnesses which may have affected you and your family, and the areas you have lived in or in which you were born. Find one or two charities which might consider helping you. Write and ask for a grant to cover your mortgage arrears. Explain that you and your family are threatened with eviction and homelessness, that you will be able to make your full mortgage payments in future, and that this single payment will enable you to keep your home.

Ask your lender to 'capitalise' your mortgage arrears

This means that they will add the amount of your arrears to the capital you still owe and arrange for you to repay this higher amount as a new mortgage. Your lender might be more willing to consider this if you can show that you have already tried other ways of raising a lump sum.

If arrears of mortgage interest are capitalised and they exceed 12 months arrears or £1,000, whichever is the greater, *and* no arrangements to reduce the arrears have been made, the lender has to inform the Inland Revenue who may take your loan out of the MIRAS system (see page 10). Tax relief on interest would then have to be claimed direct from the Inland Revenue.

However, if satisfactory arrangements have been made to reduce arrears even where capitalised interest exceeds 12 months arrears or £1,000, the lender does not have to notify the Inland Revenue.

For loans taken out before 1 August 1988, the limit of 12 months arrears or £1,000 extends to each borrower if the loan is in joint names, unless the joint borrowers are married. For loans taken out after 1 August 1988 in the names of joint borrowers who are not married, the single limit will apply.

If you are on income support you should be getting at least some help towards mortgage interest payments. However, if additional arrears have built up while you have been on benefit (eg, you have been paid the money for mortgage interest but spent it on other essential outgoings), the DHSS will not help with interest payments now due in respect of those arrears. You should be entitled to some additional income support to help pay the interest due on the 50 per cent of your mortgage payments that the DHSS did not help with during your first 16 weeks on benefit, provided you continued claiming benefit after 16 weeks.

Important Never take out another mortgage in order to pay off arrears on your present one. If you cannot pay one mortgage, how will you pay two?

Increasing your monthly payments

Work out carefully how much extra you could afford to pay your lender each month over and above your mortgage repayments. Check Chapters Three and Four to make sure that your income is as high as possible. Check Chapter Two to make sure that your mortgage costs are as low as possible. Encourage your lender to agree to any rearrangements you can suggest, by pointing out that the reduction in your mortgage costs will give you spare cash each month to put towards your mortgage arrears.

Some lenders may agree to accept interest only and suspend the capital part of your repayments while you are trying to clear arrears. You can pay what would have been the capital part of the payment (and a bit extra if you can afford it) towards clearing the arrears.

Negotiating with your lender(s)

If you have more than one mortgage in arrears and cannot raise enough to cover them all, do not repay one in full and leave yourself unable to offer any money to the other(s). Try and spread what you have raised among them. When you share it out you may have to give more to the lender to whom you owe the most or who is the most advance in their legal proceedings against you.

If you cannot make a lump sum payment to clear all your arrears, you will have to pay off the remaining amount in monthly instalments. Work out how much you can afford each month and how many months it would take you to clear the arrears if you repaid at this rate. Your lender will be pressing you to clear the arrears in as short a time as possible. They may suggest a time limit which would mean higher instalments than you could afford. Do not agree to this. Write to your lender stating what you can pay each month and start paying this immediately. Your lender may not be satisfied, but remember that if they take you to court your regular payments will help convince the judge that you made your offer in good faith.

IF YOU CANNOT CLEAR YOUR ARREARS

If the offer you make is not accepted in court, your lender will be granted a possession order. After you have been evicted by the bailiffs, the lender will sell your home, take what is owed from the proceeds, deduct legal and estate agent's fees, repay any other lenders in the order in which they registered their charges, and give you what is left over. It would be a good idea to ask the court at the hearing, even though they have granted possession to the lender, to allow you time to sell your home yourself. If you were to sell on the open market you might be able to get a higher price for your home than your lender would.

If your debts are greater than the value of your home, you face the risk of being made bankrupt. If this happens, all your possessions, including your home, will be taken over by a person called the Official Receiver, who will be responsible for raising as much as possible from the sale to repay your lenders or creditors. Being bankrupt means that you cannot trade under your name, you cannot have a bank account and sign cheques, and you cannot get credit. These restrictions are only lifted when you can discharge yourself from bankruptcy, either by paying off all your debts or, after you have been bankrupt for some time, by convincing the bankruptcy court that, although you cannot repay your debts, it would be reasonable to agree to your discharge. If you are going to be declared bankrupt, there is no point in trying to sell your home. Stay where you are, but let the local authority know that you and your family are about to be evicted and made homeless.

Special note for separating partners If your partner is declared bankrupt, you should get legal advice to establish the rights you have to the home as against those of your partner's creditors.

CHAPTER SEVEN

Separation

If you and your partner are separating, you may need a solicitor to help you negotiate what your share in the home will be, possibly through the court. This section explains how you can try to keep your home in the long term and how to make sure that you do not lose it before a final settlement is made.

IF YOU ARE MARRIED *OR* IF YOUR HOME IS JOINTLY OWNED

- ☐ **You do not have to leave your home** unless your partner gets a court order which rules that you should leave, or the lender obtains a court order for possession.
- ☐ **Never agree to the sale of your home** until you have looked at all the possible options. If you are getting advice from a solicitor or advice centre, they may not be aware of the many ways of increasing your income (see Chapters Three and Four) or reducing your housing costs (see Chapter Two) which might enable you to keep your home. If you are not happy with the advice you have been given, get a second opinion and ask for an explanation of anything you do not understand.
- ☐ **Act quickly.** The longer you leave doing anything about your home and mortgage, the more difficult it will be to keep it.
- ☐ Do not be put off by the thought of **high legal costs**. You may get legal aid and have to pay nothing at all (see Appendix 9).

WHAT TO DO IN THE SHORT TERM

Until a final agreement has been made which decides the property rights of you and your partner, you must decide where you want to live, and ensure that your partner does not borrow money against the property or sell your home without telling you.

Rights of occupation

You will always have the right to remain in your home in the short term, but you may not want to do this. The possibilities open to you are outlined below.

- ☐ If your partner is happy to leave, you can obviously stay in your home, but you must make sure that the mortgage and other payments are being kept up. See page 92 for what to do if you are taking over that responsibility.
- ☐ If you both want to remain in the home, you can both try to stay there until a property settlement has been agreed. If this is not possible, you can try to get your partner out by taking legal action. Your legal rights, and how quickly you can enforce them, depend very much on whether you are married to your partner, on who owns the property and on how your partner has behaved towards you and your children if you have any.

If there has been violence or unreasonable behaviour

The Acts mentioned in this section apply equally to women and men. However, as it is normally women who need to apply for protection using this legislation, this section has been written from their point of view.

- ☐ **If you are not married** and your partner owns the home (or you own it jointly) you will only be able to get him out if he has behaved violently, or in such a way as to have caused distress to you and/or the children. You will have to provide evidence of this.

  You can seek an injunction under the Domestic Violence and Matrimonial Proceedings Act 1976 in any County Court. The injunction can order your former partner not to molest you or any children living with you (this is called a 'non-molestation order'), and can exclude him from the home or a specified area around it (an 'ouster order'). If you have been forced to leave, the injunction can order your partner to let you return. Note that ouster orders are not normally granted for longer than three months in the first instance.

□ **If you are married** to your partner, your rights to exclude him are much more extensive.

(a) You can apply for an injunction under the Domestic Violence Act just as an unmarried woman can in the circumstances described above.

(b) You can apply for (i) a 'personal protection order' and (ii) an 'exclusion order' in the Magistrates' Court under the Domestic Violence Proceedings and Magistrates' Court Act 1978. However, to obtain (i) you must establish actual or threatened violence, and to obtain (ii) you must establish actual violence. Moreover, the orders that can be made are more limited than those under the Domestic Violence Act. The court procedure, however, is simpler than that under the Domestic Violence Act.

(c) A spouse has rights to the matrimonial house even if it is in the other spouse's name. These rights are given by the Matrimonial Homes Act 1983. In addition, the Act gives the court power to exclude either spouse from the matrimonial home. You can seek an ouster order—normally from the County Court—to exclude your husband from the matrimonial home. In deciding whether to grant the order, the court will look at the conduct of the parties, their respective needs and financial resources, the needs of any children and other relevant factors. An application under the Matrimonial Homes Act will normally be made where divorce or judicial separation proceedings have already started, although this is not essential. However, if in addition to an ouster order you wish to obtain a non-molestation order to protect you and/or your children, you *will* have to start proceedings for divorce or judicial separation if you have not already done so.

As you can see, the law in this area is rather complicated and it will be essential for you to obtain legal advice as to the best course of action.

Although you may have a long-term right to remain in your home and intend to pursue that right, injunctions are not always kept, and you may have to leave your home anyway, or need somewhere else to stay while an injunction is being arranged. The choices open to you are limited.

- ☐ You can ask your local authority for temporary accommodation under the Housing Act 1985 Part III. This says that local authorities have a duty to find accommodation for any women with dependent children homeless because of violence or the threat of it. You may be asked for evidence of the violence, for example from a doctor or health visitor. If there is no evidence, the local authority may not help you as they may say that you can continue to live in your home. If the local authority give you temporary accommodation, they may try to insist that you should apply for an injunction to make your home 'safe' to return to. You do not have to do this, but you will need help to argue with the local authority. You can get this help from a housing advice centre, SHAC, a Women's Aid Refuge, or a local advice centre (see Appendix 10).

- ☐ You can go and stay with friends or relatives. But, if this arrangement can only last for a few days, you will probably find yourself in the position outlined in the previous paragraph.

- ☐ You can go to a Women's Aid Refuge. Any woman can go to a refuge for advice. Refuges can also provide accommodation for women at risk of violence. Their addresses are kept confidential to protect the women living there, but can be obtained from the Women's Aid Federation, citizens advice bureaux, social services departments, SHAC or the police (see Appendix 10). If you have to leave your home for fear of domestic violence, you can continue to claim a rate rebate and/or income support towards the mortgage interest, as well as your housing costs on your present home.

- ☐ If you leave the home you own, or jointly own, because of a breakdown in your relationship, the DHSS and the local authority housing benefit office will ignore your share of the value of the house for at least 26 weeks in working out how much capital you have. If you make efforts to sell the home, or take legal action to allow you to move back in, then it can be ignored for longer. See Appendix 6 for more details.

Preventing the sale of your home or a reduction of your share in it

Whether you are living in your home or not, it is vital to take any necessary steps to protect your rights to live in the home and to your share in the value of the home by making sure that your partner does not try to raise another mortgage or sell your home without telling you. If your partner does raise another mortgage, ie, s/he borrows on the security of the home, this will inevitably reduce the value of the equity, and may also increase the risk of lenders applying for repossession of the home if your partner defaults on the additional payments.

If you are married

If the property is in both names, neither of you can sell or borrow money without the other's signature. However, whilst this is technically the case, to avoid any possibility of your signature being used without your consent, it may be as well to request that all your documents are dealt with via your solicitor if you have one.

If the property is in your spouse's sole name, you will have to 'register a charge' to show that you are claiming an interest in the property. This, in effect, stops the property being sold because your interest overrides any transactions made *after* your charge has been registered. You can get your solicitor to do this, and legal aid is available, but registering a charge is quite simple and you can do it yourself.

- ☐ **Registering a charge** Buy Land Registry Form No. 96 at a law stationers (this is relatively inexpensive). Law stationers are listed in the Yellow Pages. Fill in the form and write across the top, 'This search is being made for the purpose of the Matrimonial Homes Act 1983'. Post it to your District Land Registry Office. The Central Land Registry (Lincolns Inn Fields, London WC2 (01-405 3488)), publishes an address list of District Land Registry offices and the areas they cover. They will tell you if your home is registered at the Land Registry and what the Title Number is.
- ☐ **If it is registered** Buy and complete Land Registry Form 99 and send it with the necessary (small) fee to the Chief Land Registrar at the same District Land Registry Office as before.
- ☐ **If it is not registered (unregistered)** You will have to register what is known as a Class F Charge at the Land Charges Registry. Again, all you will have to do is to complete a form. Buy Land Charges Form K2, complete it and post it to the Land

Charges Department, Burrington Way, Plymouth. This will register a charge on the property.

If you are divorcing

If you divorce, and the court makes an order allowing you to continue to live in the matrimonial home and the property is still in your husband's name, you must renew your registration (see section above) as soon as possible. To do this, buy, complete and send either Land Registry Form 100 (if the land is registered) or Land Charges Form K13 (if the land is unregistered).

It sometimes happens that a divorce is to be completed before the court has decided the long-term division of the property. If this happens to you, you must get, from the court, before your divorce is made absolute, permission to re-register your 'right to occupy' after the divorce is finalised. You must then, of course, make sure that your right is registered by your solicitor or by you.

Remember a charge only protects you:

- ☐ while you are married; if you are divorcing, see above;
- ☐ from your husband selling the property. If there are mortgage arrears, the lender has first claim on the property and can sell. However, you can negotiate to take over the mortgage yourself (see page 92).
- ☐ in your matrimonial home. If your husband owns more than one property, you can only register a charge on the one you have been living in.

If you are not married

If you both own your home, you have equal rights to live there until the court decides on long-term ownership. Neither of you can borrow more money on mortgage or sell the home without the other's signature.

If your home is in your partner's name only, you may be able to protect the value of your share by starting court proceedings under Section 30 of the Law of Property Act 1925 and immediately registering a 'pending action'. You will have to seek legal advice on how to start the proceedings and register a pending action. You will only succeed if you can show that you have contributed to the purchase of or improvements to the property.

See also page 82 on injunctions.

WHAT TO DO IN THE LONG TERM

You and your partner have to decide how to share your property and money. If you can come to an agreement through your solicitor then the court will be asked to approve that agreement. In cases of dispute, the court has the power to decide. If you want to remain in your home you must make this quite clear to your solicitor. You may be worried that you will not be able to afford to pay the mortgage(s), but most people can cut their costs or increase their income in some of the ways described on pages 11-59. Check these carefully. You may have to convince your solicitor as well as yourself about them all.

This section explains the legal guidelines which the court and your solicitor will be bearing in mind. It is important that you know about them.

You may also be worried that your home is in need of repair. At the time of any re-mortgage you should ask your lender for the money needed to keep or put your home in good condition (see page 68). Check whether you may be entitled to a grant from your local authority (see Chapter Five).

If you are married

If you are separating you will probably be applying for a divorce or judicial separation. When granting either of these the court also has to make a decision about property, money and children. The general guidelines for assessing what you will receive are given in the Matrimonial Causes Act 1973 (as amended). It says that first consideration will be given to the children of the marriage. In addition, the court has wide powers to take into account all the circumstances of the case including, for example, the income and needs of both partners and the contribution they have made to the welfare of the family.

If you do not want to get divorced, you can still apply to the court to have your share of the property assessed under the Married Women's Property Act 1882.

How the court decides

The court can order almost any arrangement it wishes, provided it is fair to both parties. It is therefore important that your solicitor asks for all you want, and are entitled to. The court must consider whether it is appropriate to end the financial relationship between the two parties to a marriage to help the parties make a 'clean break'. There are no rigid rules to decide what share of the value of the home you should have, and what the level of maintenance should be. You do not have to accept the first offer that your solicitor recommends to you. It may be possible to negotiate, or to persuade the court to order, a better arrangement.

If you want to stay in your home.

Note: the following sections are written from the woman's point of view, but the law in this area applies equally to men.

There are three main options for you if you wish to stay in your home.

- ☐ **Have the home transferred to your name and in exchange accept reduced maintenance or no maintenance at all**. This is called a property transfer. You would be asking for your partner's share of the property to be transferred to you and in exchange would make concessions as to the level of maintenance you would accept for yourself and/or your children. In most cases, you will now have to pay the mortgage, although if your husband is paying any maintenance the court can order that a specific proportion is used to meet the capital part of your monthly mortgage repayments.

  Points to consider

  (a) Maintenance is only useful if you actually receive it. If your husband is unlikely to pay regularly or at all, you could be much better off with full ownership of your home. This sort of settlement fits in with the idea of the 'clean break' outlined above. It is, however, always worthwhile to get an order for even a token sum, for example £1 per year, as you can then apply to have the order varied if your husband's circumstances change for the better. If you do not have an order, this cannot be raised.

  (b) If you are claiming income support your maintenance together with any other income (eg, part-time earnings, family credit, child benefit) will be deducted from your income support payment. If your maintenance is higher than your income support entitlement, you do not get income support and have to rely on your maintenance. Unless you are sure that the agreed maintenance payments will be paid regularly, you may be better off with a property transfer, low maintenance and some help from income support. It may also be possible for your maintenance to be paid directly to the DHSS by the court if there are likely to be difficulties. You will then get the full amount of your maintenance and income support regularly.

(c) You may find it helpful to get a letter from your solicitor stating that your husband is fulfilling his obligations to maintain you by giving you capital (in the form of a home) to avoid you becoming homeless, instead of giving you higher maintenance payments. Unless the DHSS accepts this, they may take your husband to court for failing to maintain you.

☐ **Have the property transferred to your name and raise the money to pay your husband his share.** The court will decide what proportion of equity this is. (See page 2 for a definition of 'equity'.)

Points to consider

The best place to try for a mortgage in your name is your present building society, bank or local authority. *Never* go to a finance company for a mortgage, as they charge high interest rates, and if you stop paying, the debt mounts up very quickly.

☐ **Stay in the property until some future event, such as when you want to move or remarry.** In this case, the property is sold and you receive what the court decides would be your share. If your husband pays the mortgage while you do this, you will get less maintenance.

Points to consider

(i) Some agreements of this sort decide that the house will be sold when your children are grown up. This is usually a bad idea, because your children may no longer be dependent and therefore the local authority may not give you any help with housing after you have sold your home. When you are older it may also be difficult for you to raise a large enough mortgage to buy again.

(b) **Legal aid charges**. You will probably have had legal aid to help you through your divorce proceedings and property settlement. If you 'recover or preserve' property of any value, some of the cost of your legal aid can be reclaimed by the Law Society (see Appendix 9). If your property settlement means you will be getting a cash settlement which you intend to use to buy again, you must be careful to take account of any legal fees you have to repay when you decide how much cash to accept.

If you do not want to stay in your home see Chapter Eight.

If you are already divorced

You may feel that you could have come to a more satisfactory arrangement at the time of your divorce if you had considered the alternatives more carefully. However, only if your own or your ex-husband's circumstances have changed will you be able to apply to the court to alter the property settlement. What you may then be able to do depends on the Act used for your property settlement and the length of time since your divorce. If the property was apportioned under the 1882 Act (see page 87) you can only go back to court to claim more of the value of the home within 3 years after the divorce became absolute. Under the Matrimonial Causes Act 1973 you can reapply at any time.

In a very few cases, orders will be final where the court has ordered a 'clean break'. The court is only likely to do this where there are no dependent children. In these cases, the court may dismiss your application for maintenance and say that you cannot reapply, or it may order maintenance for a limited period, and say that you cannot come back to extend the order. The power of the court to order a 'clean break' even if one party does not agree is given by the Matrimonial and Family Proceedings Act 1984.

If you had no property settlement at the time of your divorce you may be able to apply under the Matrimonial Homes and Property Act 1981, provided neither of you has remarried. If one of you has remarried, you can apply under the Married Women's Property Act 1882 to declare your interest in your property, but this must be done within three years of the Decree Absolute.

If you are not married

Married people are covered by special matrimonial legislation protecting their property rights and providing means of settling disputes on the break-up of a relationship. If you are not married, at the moment you have only limited protection and must rely on the general law of property. In 1989, however, it is expected that the court will be given the power to make a decision about property for unmarried couples whose relationship has broken down, if they have children. These powers are contained in the Family Law Reform Act 1988.

Where the home is jointly owned

If the home is jointly owned, you have a clear right to share its value. However, at the moment the court cannot order that it is transferred into your name; it can only decide the proportion each party owns and order the sale or postponed sale. In 1989, it should also be possible to have the home transferred into your name.

If you want to stay in your home, you can:

- ☐ Raise the money to buy your partner out. See Chapters Three and Four for how to increase your income and Chapter Two for how to lower your mortgage costs. Then ask your building society or local authority for a new mortgage.
- ☐ Try to postpone the sale. You could try to argue that the sale of your home should be postponed if you have children as the property was intended as a home for them. The court has the power under Section 30 of the Law of Property Act 1925 to postpone the sale if 'any person interested' applies.

Where the home is solely owned by your partner

At the moment, you have no automatic right to any part of the home even if your relationship has lasted a long time and there are children. You can try, however, to establish some rights.

- ☐ You will have to show that you contributed financially to the home or made a substantial direct contribution such as helping to build or improve it. It is sometimes difficult to prove you have contributed directly to the property and if you want to claim a share in the equity you should contact a solicitor for advice.

- Even if you fail to establish a financial interest in your home, you may be able to extend the time in which you can live in it, by convincing the court that the purpose of your partner in setting up the home was to provide for you and any children.
- In 1989, you should be able to have the property transferred into your name if you have children, or into your child/children's name(s).

HOW TO NEGOTIATE WITH YOUR LENDER

So far your legal rights to the home as against your partner's have been described. But if there is a mortgage on the home and you are hoping to keep on paying it yourself in the future, you will also need to negotiate with your lender to obtain their agreement to your plans. The attitude of your lender will probably vary depending on whether or not the mortgage is now in arrears.

If there are no mortgage arrears

If you have no arrears and want to try to make the payments in future you must write to your lender and explain the position. Ask them to agree to make any arrangements which would help you financially as described in Chapter Two, and to give you time to make them. If you are hoping that ownership of the home will be transferred to you as part of a divorce or property settlement, explain that to your lender.

Problems

Sometimes people find that lenders will not accept mortgage payments from them. Even if your lender will not accept you as the borrower, pay the instalments and keep a record of your payments. This will be important if you need to show the court that you are acting in good faith. As well as sending payments you should point out any legal rights under family or property law that you have or are claiming. These will depend on whose name the home is now in and whose name is on the mortgage deed.

- **If the home and mortgage deed are in your name** then, as owner, you are entitled to make the payments and it should be sufficient to point this out.

- ☐ **If the home and mortgage deed are in your spouse's name**, then you are entitled under Section 1(5) of the Matrimonial Homes Act 1983 to make the payments in their place, and you should draw your lender's attention to this Act.
- ☐ **If the home and mortgage are in your partner's name and you are not married**, then you will need to ask your solicitor whether you have any legal rights to a part of the home under Section 30 of the Law of Property Act 1925. This right would be based on any money you have paid towards buying the home or on any work that you have put into repairing or improving it. If you do have grounds for claiming a share in the home, then tell your lender that you are taking action to establish this and ask them to accept your payments in the meantime.

If the mortgage is in arrears now

If the mortgage is in arrears now, the lender may already have started taking action against you or your partner or against you both. The action the lender will take, and what you can do to stop the action is explained in Chapter Six. Whatever stage the proceedings have reached, you may still be able to keep your home. You can try to clear the mortgage arrears (see Chapter Six). You should ask your lender to postpone any further action until after the court has decided on the property settlement. Start to pay the mortgage instalments as soon as you find out there are arrears. If you cannot afford the whole monthly payment to start with, send as much as you can with a letter explaining your situation.

CHAPTER EIGHT

How to find another home

This section describes the different types of alternative accommodation available and how to go about finding them if there is no way you can keep your present home. It can be difficult to find alternative accommodation, so *never agree to the sale of your home until you definitely have somewhere else to live.*

The first part of this chapter explains how to decide whether or not you could buy again and how to go about it. If you want to do this, look carefully at Chapter Seven to see how you should ask for the proceeds from the sale of your present home to be split up. The other parts of this chapter deal with trying to get rented accommodation: from a local authority; a housing association; a private landlord or in a new town.

If all of these fail and the court orders the sale of your home, your local authority may have to help to prevent you from becoming homeless. It is important that you contact your local authority as soon as possible. They may only be able to register your name on the housing waiting list, but they may also have an advice centre which can help you with your mortgage difficulties. Contact the authority immediately if you think you *may* become homeless.

BUY AGAIN

If you have enough cash from the sale of your former home, it may be possible for you to buy again. If you have had difficulties in paying for your present home you must make sure that you do not have the same problems again. Consider buying a smaller, cheaper property (but not one in a poor state of repair), so that you will need a smaller mortgage. You could also consider a shared ownership scheme; these schemes are run by local authorities and housing associations.

Some building societies are now offering index-linked mortgages which are cheaper than conventional repayment mortgages. These mortgages are generally only available to first-time buyers. If your previous mortgage was in your partner's name you would probably be classed as a first-time buyer; even if your previous mortgage was in your joint names you may still be eligible.

Can you afford to buy again?

To decide whether or not you can buy again, you will need to find out how much a suitable home will cost and how much you can borrow.

How much can you pay?

The amount you can pay depends on the amount of capital you have and on the amount you can borrow on mortgage.

- ☐ **How much capital can you raise?** Calculate how much you will have left over after the sale of your present home. You will first need to find out the value of your present home (by asking two or three local estate agents what price you could hope to get). You will then have to find out the amount that you still owe (by asking your lenders for redemption figures, see page 18), the cost of selling (by getting estimates of the fees which will be charged by your estate agent, solicitor and removal firm), and the cost of buying again (by asking the solicitor for an estimate of the fee and putting aside a bit extra in case you have to pay for repairs to your new home). Deduct these costs from the value of your home to see how much capital you can rely on having left over. Any capital you have left over after the sale of your present home will be ignored by the DHSS for up to 6 months, when your eligibility for income support will be assessed. This is the case so long as you are going to use it to buy another home.

  Note: if you are divorcing and have had legal aid to help with court costs, you may have to pay backsome of the capital to the Law Society: see Appendix 9.

- ☐ **How much can you borrow on a mortgage?** This will depend on your income. You will have to give all the lenders who might grant you a mortgage the figures for your gross annual income and that of your partner. Ask them how much they are prepared to lend in principle. If you are not working it is possible to raise a mortgage on the basis of your income from income support. But remember that income support will only cover the interest payments not the capital or any insurance premium. For the first 16 weeks on benefit only 50 per cent of the interest will be met by your income support (see page 47) and the DHSS can restrict any interest payments they think are excessive (see page 49).

If you are selling your present home because you have fallen behind with your mortgage payments and have been unable to clear the arrears, you may well find it difficult to persuade your lender to grant you another mortgage. You will, however, be able to make a good case for getting another mortgage if you can show that the reason for the arrears will not occur again, for example, the cause for the arrears was the breakdown of your marriage or an illness from which you have now recovered. If this is not possible, you will probably have to pay cash or you will not be able to buy again.

How much will a suitable home cost?

Now that you know how much you can pay, find out if there is any chance of your getting a suitable home by looking in local newspapers and by contacting local estate agents. Although flats may appear cheaper than houses, it is worth remembering that you will probably have to pay a share of repair costs. Be very wary of blocks of flats with high service charges.

How to raise a mortgage

If you will not have enough capital from the sale of your home to buy another home outright, you will have to consider how you can raise a mortgage.

Who can you borrow from?

The different types of lenders are described on pages 7-9. The cheapest arrangements are offered by building societies, local authorities and banks so you should only consider approaching them. A local authority will usually only lend to someone who is buying for the first time. You could be classed as a first-time buyer if you have separated from your partner and are now hoping to buy on your own. A local authority may also be able to nominate you to a building society under the support scheme (see below).

If you do not fall into the category to whom a local authority will lend money but you are threatened with homelessness and cannot raise a mortgage, ask them to make an exception for you, using their powers under Section 435 of the Housing Act 1984, Part XIV. Building societies are the most common source of money for people who are buying their home for the second time. If your previous lender was a building society or if you have savings in a building society, contact that one first. If they refuse, see your local authority for help under the support scheme. This is a special arrangement that many local authorities have with building societies in their area. The local authority can provide you with a letter of introduction to one of the support scheme societies. That society will then consider your application for a mortgage, even though you may not have been saving with that society. Most support schemes are for first-time buyers only. If you were a joint owner with your former partner ask to be treated as a first-time buyer. Your case will be stronger if you can show that the old mortgage was based largely on your partner's income.

Many banks are now granting mortgages but they, like building societies, are likely to be wary of someone who has been in difficulties in the past.

If you have tried all these options and been refused, you can ask an estate agent, solicitor, bank manager or mortgage broker to refer you to a building society. Be very careful to check whether you will be charged a fee for this introduction and make sure that you are not obliged to take a very expensive form of mortgage. If the broker fails to get you a suitable mortgage they are only allowed to charge £1 (Consumer Credit Act 1974). Brokers can, however, charge for any surveys etc, carried out on your behalf.

What type of mortgage should you get?

The different types of mortgage and the way you can get government help with your payments are described on pages 1-10. Briefly, if you want the lowest possible monthly payments you should try and obtain a capital repayment mortgage from a building society, bank or local authority.

How to apply for your mortgage if you are working

Write to the lender you have decided to approach first, stating:

- ☐ that you would like a capital repayment mortgage, and in whose name(s) it should be;
- ☐ your gross income and that of your partner (if any) and how they are made up. Give details of your basic pay, your regular over-time and bonuses, and any pay rise you are to receive in the near future;
- ☐ the amount of capital you can put to the purchase price;
- ☐ that you have calculated that you will be able to meet the mortgage payments (see Appendix 2) as well as your other commitments. Show that you have considered such costs as travelling to work and child-minding;
- ☐ why your circumstances led to your selling your last home and why any difficulties you had then will not crop up again. If you are asking someone other than your previous lender for this mortgage, you will have to explain why your previous lender was not willing to help you.

How to apply for your mortgage if you are receiving income support

(i) Write to the manager of the DHSS office in the areas where you are hoping to buy, stating:

- ☐ that you are now receiving income support. Give the address of your present office and your number;
- ☐ that you have to leave your present home and are hoping to buy again to avoid becoming homeless;
- ☐ that you would like a letter confirming that the manager will, in principle, be prepared to include in your benefit the interest payments on any mortgage you raise within a reasonable limit. Say that you need this letter so you can show your lender how the mortgage interest payments will be made.

(ii) Write to the lender you have decided to approach, stating:

- ☐ that you would like a capital repayment mortgage;
- ☐ that you are enclosing a copy of the letter you have received from the DHSS to show how the mortgage interest payments will be made;
- ☐ that, once you have found a suitable property and know the exact amount of mortgage you will need, you will get a further letter from the DHSS agreeing to meet the whole or part of the interest payments on that amount;
- ☐ *either* that you will meet the capital payments and explain how you will do this (see page 51 for ways to try), *or* that you would like the lender to waive the capital part of the mortgage until you are in a position to start making them. Explain how and when this might be;
- ☐ the amount of capital you can put to the purchase price;
- ☐ why your circumstances led to the sale of your last home and why any difficulties you had before will not happen again. If you are asking someone other than your previous lender for a mortgage, you will have to explain why your previous lender would not help.

(iii) When you have found the home you want to buy, write to the DHSS again stating the amount of mortgage you need. Ask for a letter confirming that they will revise your weekly benefit to cover the interest payments on this amount.

How to get a guarantor for your mortgage

As a condition of granting the mortgage your lender may insist that you provide a guarantor. A guarantor is someone who agrees to make the mortgage payments if you should fail to do so. If you are unable to provide a guarantor you may find your lender will not press for one, especially if other negotiations are going smoothly. You can ask either an individual or the local authority to act as a guarantor for you. For a person to be acceptable to a lender they must have assets greater in value than your mortgage (eg, their own home) or have enough income after paying their own rent/mortgage to be able to pay yours if necessary. Local authorities have powers under two different Acts to stand as guarantor:

- ☐ they can guarantee your mortgage payments and any extension of them under Section 442 of the Housing Act 1985 Part XIV; *or*
- ☐ the social services department can guarantee your mortgage payments if you have children under 16. They are only likely to consider this if it will prevent your family from becoming homeless.

Appeals

If you feel your lender's insistence on a guarantor is unreasonable because you have shown how you can meet the mortgage repayments, or if your building society or local authority are not being very helpful, it may be possible to appeal against their decision (see page 18).

RENTED ACCOMMODATION

If you cannot raise a mortgage, there may be other ways of finding accommodation for your family. They are described very briefly below.

Private rented accommodation

This is always difficult to find, especially if you have children, and it is very often furnished which will mean little or no storage space for any furnishings you may have already acquired. Unfurnished, privately-rented accommodation is scarce. Local shop windows, newspapers and accommodation agencies are the main sources of information. However, always get advice before signing any agreements or paying any fees. You will probably have to have money for returnable deposits and rent in advance. After January 1989, when the Housing Act 1988 comes into force, you may also have to find money for premiums ('key money'). If you are on income support you may be able to claim money for rent in advance from the social fund. However, the money will be in the form of a loan (you will have to pay it back from your weekly benefit). It is also fairly unlikely that the social fund officer will agree to pay it to you, because other forms of loan are given higher priority, but it is still worth applying. The loan would be for a maximum of four times the weekly rent.

Housing Associations

Housing Associations currently have unfurnished properties at fair rents. In 1989, however, their rents are likely to go up. This is because of the changes that will be made by the Housing Act 1988.

Housing associations can rarely help at short notice, but may be prepared to put your name on a waiting list. If their lists are closed, you will probably only be considered if you are put forward (nominated) by your local authority or another referral agency.

In some circumstances, housing associations can buy your home and either leave you in it or rehouse you elsewhere. You will get less for your home than if you sell it on the open market, because an occupied house is worth less than an empty one. However, you will be getting somewhere to live out of the arrangement. If you do this, you must make sure that you will get enough money to clear all your debts.

Your local authority or citizens advice bureau may be able to give you the names of housing associations in your area.

APPROACH YOUR LOCAL HOUSING AUTHORITY

Your local authority may be able to help you in a number of ways, so go to them as soon as possible and explain your situation. They may:

- ☐ **give you advice**. Many local authorities have housing advice centres where people can be helped to sort out their difficulties;
- ☐ **rehouse you**. They may only be able to put your name on a waiting list, but you should do this even if there seems no immediate need. Different local authorities have different policies on helping people in mortgage difficulties, so ask what they might do for you;
- ☐ **grant you a new mortgage**. See page 8 for details of local authority mortgages;
- ☐ **accept you as homeless and rehouse you**.

HOMELESSNESS AND LOCAL AUTHORITIES

If you are already homeless or are likely to become homeless within 28 days after you report your situation to your local authority, then you have certain legal rights under the Housing (Homeless Persons) Act 1977 (now the Housing Act 1985, Part III).

This puts a legal obligation on local authorities to provide accommodation for people who fulfil certain conditions. The following points detail these conditions, and suggest what action you should take.

- ☐ **You are homeless**. Go to your local authority as soon as you know that you will be homeless. They have a duty to begin investigations if you will be homeless within 28 days and *must* provide accommodation if you are actually homeless and are in priority need.
- ☐ **You are in priority need**, ie, you have dependent children; you are pregnant; you are over retirement age; you are vulnerable because of illness or disability; you are homeless bcause of fire or flood.
- ☐ **You did not make yourself homeless intentionally.** You are intentionally homeless if you deliberately do, or fail to do, something which results in your homelessness. However, if your homelessness results from something done in good faith or because you were unaware that there were any alternatives, you should not be judged intentionally homeless. The Code of Guidance to the Housing Act 1985, Part III paragraph 215 says:

> A person who chooses to sell his home, or who has lost it because of wilful and persistent refusal to pay rent, would in most cases be regarded as having become homeless intentionally. Authorities should in such cases be satisfied that the person has taken the action which has led to the loss of accommodation with full knowledge of the likely consequences. Where, however, a person was obliged to sell because he could not keep up the mortgage repayments, or got into rent arrears, because of real personal or financial difficulties, or because he was incapable of managing his affairs on account of, eg, old age or mental illness, his acts or omissions should not be regarded as having been deliberate. Where homelessness is the result of serious financial difficulties arising, for example, from

> loss of employment or greatly reduced earning, the applicant should not normally be regarded as intentionally homeless. A spouse or cohabitee should not automatically be held to be jointly responsible for rent or mortgage arrears incurred by the other partner; the authority should make inquiries with a view to establishing whether responsibility for the arrears was shared in practice before treating the applicant as intentionally homeless. An owner occupier, inescapably faced with foreclosure, who sells before the mortgagee recovers possession through the courts, should not on that account be treated as intentionally homeless.

This Code does not have the same force as the Act, but it might be helpful to your case.

But, even if you are intentionally homeless, you are entitled to accommodation for a reasonable period if you are in priority need.

If you are homeless or about to become homeless, contact one of the organisations listed in Appendix 10 for advice.

There are a number of additional points to remember.

- ☐ Your local authority is responsible for your furniture as well as for you, even if they have to put you in temporary accommodation.
- ☐ Your local authority must provide accommodation if you need it until they have completed any necessary investigation.
- ☐ You are entitled to written notification of any decision they take about you under this Act. If the decision is unfavourable, the local authority must state their reasons. If this happens to you, it may be possible to challenge the decision, so get advice.

Tax allowances and child benefit

THE MAIN TAX ALLOWANCES FOR TAX YEAR APRIL 1988/89

		£
Single person		2,605
Married man		4,095
Working wife	up to	2,605
Additional personal allowance for looking after children		1,490

Note: For the tax year 1988/89, the rate of tax is 25% up to £19,300 with higher rates for income above that level.

CHILD BENEFIT AND ONE PARENT BENEFIT FOR APRIL 1988/89

	£
Child benefit for each child	£7.25
One parent benefit	4.90

How to work out your mortgage repayments

HOW TO WORK OUT YOUR MONTHLY CAPITAL AND INTEREST PAYMENTS

The tables printed below will enable you to work out the total monthly cost of mortgages of different amounts over different terms. The monthly payments include interest and capital.

Note that the longer the term, the lower the repayment. This is because repayment of capital is spread over more years. The change from 15 to 20 years makes more difference than the change from 25 to 30 years.

Monthly payments of capital and interest at 11.5%

Because the government subsidy is based on a tax rate of 25%, the actual interest you pay is 25% lower than the stated rate. At 11.5% interest, you pay 8.6%.

Mortgage	*Repayment Period*			
	15 yrs	*20 yrs*	*25 yrs*	*30 yrs*
£	£ p	£ p	£ p	£ p
50	0.50	0.44	0.41	0.39
100	1.01	0.88	0.82	0.78
200	2.02	1.76	1.64	1.56
300	3.03	2.64	2.46	2.34
400	4.04	3.52	3.28	3.12
500	5.05	4.44	4.11	3.90
1,000	10.10	8.88	8.22	7.83
2,000	20.20	17.76	16.44	15.66
3,000	30.30	26.64	24.66	23.49
4,000	40.40	35.52	32.88	31.32
5,000	50.50	44.40	41.10	39.15
6,000	60.60	53.28	49.32	46.98
10,000	101.00	88.80	82.20	78.30

If you do not pay your mortgage net of tax but make the full repayment and claim tax relief at 11.5%, your costs will be:

Mortgage	*Repayment Period*			
	15 yrs	*20 yrs*	*25 yrs*	*30 yrs*
500	5.96	5.40	5.13	4.98
1,000	11.92	10.81	10.26	9.97

Table 1

Monthly repayments at different interest rates

Because interest rates vary from time to time, this table gives the repayments for different rates of interest and different repayment periods. Each figure is the cost of paying back £1,000 per month.

		Repayment period			
Actual Rate	*Interest Rate*	*15 yrs*	*20 yrs*	*25 yrs*	*30 yrs*
%	%	£	£	£	£
10.50	7.90	9.68	8.43	7.74	7.34
11.00	8.20	9.86	8.62	7.95	7.55
11.50	8.60	10.10	8.88	8.22	7.83
12.00	9.00	10.34	9.13	8.49	8.12
12.50	9.40	10.59	9.40	8.77	8.41

Table 2

How to use the tables

Example
If you want to get a mortgage of £23,800 over 25 years at an interest rate of 11.5% (8.6% actual rate).

Over 25 years, monthly payment of £10,000	= £82.20
Over 25 years, monthly payment of £10,000	= £82.20
Over 25 years, monthly payment of £3,000	= £24.66
Over 25 years, monthly payment of £500	= £4.11
Over 25 years, monthly payments of £300	= £2.46

Total monthly repayment = £195.63

So a mortgage or £23,800 over 25 years at 11.5% would cost £195.63 a month. You could also do this calculation as:

$$\begin{aligned} 23 \times £8.22 &= £189.06 \\ + 8/10 \times £8.22 &= £6.57 \\ &= £195.63 \end{aligned}$$

If you are getting a mortgage at a different interest rate, use Table 2 to work out your monthly payments.

A mortgage of £23,800 over 25 years at an interest rate of 12% would mean paying 9% actual interest. The repayment would be £8.49 for every £1,000 per month:

$$\begin{aligned} 23 \times £8.49 &= £195.27 \\ + 8/10 \times £8.49 &= £6.79 \\ &= £202.06 \end{aligned}$$

HOW TO WORK OUT THE TOTAL WEEKLY MORTGAGE REPAYMENT

To work out the weekly mortgage repayment from the monthly figure:

- ☐ Multiply the monthly figure by 12 to get the repayment per year.
- ☐ Divide the yearly figure by 52.

$$\begin{aligned} £195.63 \times 12 &= £2,347.56 \\ £2,347.56 \div 52 &= £45.14 \end{aligned}$$

The weekly payment is therefore £45.14.

HOW TO WORK OUT THE WEEKLY MORTGAGE INTEREST PAYMENT

Suppose you owe £23,800 and are paying an actual interest rate of 8.6%

- ☐ Work out the interest you owe per year:

$$£23,800 \times 8.6\,\%$$

$$£23,800 \times \frac{8.6}{100} = £2,046.80$$

- ☐ Work out the interest you owe per week:

$$£2,046.30 \div 52 = £39.36$$

HOW TO WORK OUT THE WEEKLY MORTGAGE CAPITAL REPAYMENT

To find your weekly capital repayment you need to use the tables to get the total weekly mortgage repayment.

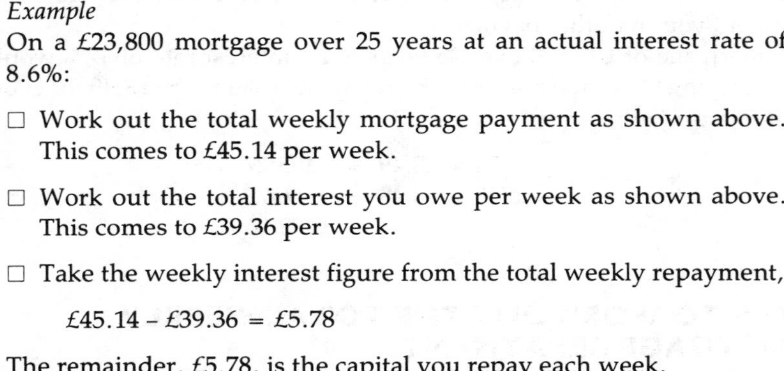

Example
On a £23,800 mortgage over 25 years at an actual interest rate of 8.6%:

- ☐ Work out the total weekly mortgage payment as shown above. This comes to £45.14 per week.
- ☐ Work out the total interest you owe per week as shown above. This comes to £39.36 per week.
- ☐ Take the weekly interest figure from the total weekly repayment,

  £45.14 – £39.36 = £5.78

The remainder, £5.78, is the capital you repay each week.

How to calculate family credit

The rates for family credit (FC) are laid down by parliament, and they are generally increased once a year. The rate in force at the date of claim will apply throughout the 6 months of the award (see page 21).

THE CALCULATION

To work out how much FC you qualify for, follow these steps:

(i) Work out the 'maximum family credit' for your family

To work this out, add together the child credits for the ages of your children, and one adult credit. (You only include one adult credit, whether you have a partner, or are a single parent.)

Adult credit	£32.10
Child credits	
Under 11	6.05
11-15	11.40
16-17	14.70
18	21.35

(ii) Work out your income

See pages 23-24 for how to do this and for what you should include in your calculation.

(iii) Compare your income with the 'threshold level'

Until April 1989 this will be £51.45.

☐ If your income is below the threshold, then you will be entitled to maximum FC (see (i) above).

☐ If your income is above the threshold:

— work out the excess over the threshold;
— calculate 70% of the excess;
— deduct this from the maximum FC to find the amount of FC that will be paid.

Example
Ms Jones is a single parent with 2 children of 12 and 10. Her net earnings are £80 per week, and she receives child benefit and one parent benefit.

Maximum family credit

Adult credit	£32.10
Child credits	
12-year-old	£11.40
10-year-old	£6.05
	£49.55

Income

Ms Jones' income = £80 per week.
(Child benefit and one parent benefit are ignored for the purpose of calculating your income.)

Final calculation

☐ Ms Jones' income is £28.55 over the threshold;

☐ 70% of this excess is £19.98;

☐ the FC payable is:

	£49.55	(maximum FC)
minus	£19.98	(70% of excess income)
	£29.57	total FC payable

How to work out your rate rebate—if you are not on income support

These figures apply until April 1989. For people not on income support (IS), the rebate calculation can be done by taking the following steps. For detailed information see CPAG's *National Welfare Benefits Handbook*.

THE REBATE CALCULATION

(i) Work out your maximum rebate

- ☐ This will normally be 80% of your general rates. Do not include water rates in this figure. Divide the annual figure by 52 to get your weekly maximum rebate
- ☐ Deduct £3.00 for each non-dependant where necessary (see page 27).

(ii) Work out your 'applicable amount'

- ☐ Use the same figures as used in Appendix 5 for IS personal allowances and premiums. The only difference is that, for rate rebates, the lone parent premium is £8.60.

(iii) Work out your net income

- ☐ Use your gross earnings, less tax, national insurance and half of any superannuation contributions. Then **ignore** the following:

—£15 if you qualify for the lone parent premium, or disability premiums (or higher pensioner premium in some cases);

—£10 if you are a member of a couple;

—£5 if you are single;

—any maintenance payments that you pay to a former partner.

- ☐ Ignore any income from lodgers and non-dependants, as well as fostering allowances and educational maintenance allowances.
- ☐ Include all social security benefits, except attendance allowance and mobility allowance.
- ☐ Include any 'tariff income' from savings over £3,000 (see page 45).

(iv) Compare your net income with your applicable amount

- ☐ If your income is less than the applicable amount then you receive the maximum rebate.
- ☐ If your income is above the applicable amount:

—work out the excess income;

—work out 20% of that excess;

—take that 20% away from the maximum rebate.

The remainder is the rebate you will receive.

Example
Mr and Mrs Brown pay general rates of £8 per week. Mr Brown gets invalidity benefit of £43.85, and Mrs Brown has net earnings of £50 per week.

Their maximum rebate is:

80% of £8.00	=	£6.40

Their applicable amount is:

personal allowance	£51.45
disability premium	£18.60
	£70.05

Their net income is:

Invalidity benefit	£43.85
net earnings (less £15 disregard)	£35.00
	£78.85

Their income is over their applicable amount by:

£8.80
–20% of £8.80 = £1.76
–deduct £1.76 from the maximum rebate (see step (i))

£6.40 – £1.76 = £4.64

Their rate rebate would be £4.64 per week.

Income support rates until April 1989

PERSONAL ALLOWANCES

These are the amounts laid down for basic living expenses. Different rates are paid for single people, couples and single parents, with additions for children according to age. A lower rate is paid for single people under 25.

Single people without children	
Under 18	£19.40
18-24	£26.05
25 or over	£33.40
Single parents	
Under 18	£19.40
18 or over	£33.40
Couples	
Both under 18	£38.80
One or both over 18	£51.45
Dependent children/young people	
Under 11	£10.75
11-15	£16.10
16-17	£19.40
18	£26.05

Premiums

These are fixed additional allowances paid to specific groups of people.

Family premium **£6.15**

You may be entitled to this premium if you have at least one child or young person living with you. You would normally have to be receiving child benefit for them. Only one premium is paid per family.

Disabled child premium **£6.15**

If you have a disabled child who is receiving attendance allowance, mobility allowance, or is registered blind you may be able to get the disabled child premium. You won't get this premium if the child has more than £3,000 in savings of his/her own. One premium is paid for each disabled child.

Lone Parent premium **£3.70**

You may be entitled to this premium if you are a single parent, and claim benefit for at least one child.

Pensioner premium **£10.65 single**
£16.25 couple

If you or your partner are between 60 and 79, you can claim this premium.

Disability premium **£13.05 single**
£18.60 couple

If you or your partner are getting attendance allowance or mobility allowance, have an invalid car, or are registered blind or are receiving invalidity benefit or severe disablement allowance, you may be entitled to this premium. You may also be entitled if you, or your partner—if they are the claimant—have been incapable for work for 28 weeks. It may be worth changing which of you is the claimant if one of you is too ill or disabled to work.

Higher Pensioner premium **£13.05 single**
£18.60 couple

You may claim this premium if either you or your partner are over 80, or one of you is over 60 and meet the conditions for the disability premium, or you or your partner were getting the disability premium within 8 weeks of your sixtieth birthday, and have been getting income support ever since.

Severe Disability premium **£24.75 single**
£49.50 couple

If you are a single claimant receiving attendance allowance, and you have no non-dependants over 18 living with you, you can claim a severe disability premium. There must also be no one claiming invalid care allowance for looking after you. For couples, both of you must be receiving attendance allowance, have no non-dependants over 18 living with you, and there must be no one claiming invalid care allowance for looking after either of you. If both of you meet these conditions, but someone receives invalid care allowance for caring for one of you, then you will still receive the single rate of premium.

Rules about savings and capital for income support, family credit and rate rebates

The rules used by the DHSS to assess your savings or capital are almost the same for the three 'income-related' benefits—income support (IS), family credit (FC) and housing benefit (HB) (rate rebate).

GENERAL RULES

If you, and your partner if you have one, have more than £6,000 in savings and capital (£8,000 for HB), you won't qualify for these benefits at all. If you have less than £3,000, it is ignored completely. Any savings between £3,000 and £6,000 (£8,000 for HB) are assumed to give you an income of £1 per week for each £250 (or part of £250) over the £3,000 figure that you have. This is called 'tariff income'.

If any of your children have savings of their own, these will also be ignored up to £3,000. Above that, you will receive no benefit for that child.

If any of your children have savings of their own, these will also be ignored up to £3,000. Above that, you will receive no benefit for that child.

WHAT IS INCLUDED IN CAPITAL?

Capital includes, amongst other things:

(i) money in bank or building society accounts;
(ii) premium bonds;
(iii) unit trusts;

(iv) stocks and shares;
(v) lump-sum redundancy payments;
(vi) savings in cash;
(vii) houses or land owned.

Capital in the form of things like shares, houses or land, is valued at its current market value. A deduction is then made to allow for the expenses of selling.

WHAT CAPITAL IS IGNORED?

Some capital is ignored, including:

(i) the value of the home you normally live in;
(ii) a property you have bought and intend to occupy within 6 months;*
(iii) money from the sale of a house which is to be used to buy another home within 6 months;*
(iv) the value of premises occupied wholly or partly by:

- ☐ your partner or a relative who is 60 or over, or disabled;
- ☐ your former partner (but not if you are divorced or estranged). An example of this situation might be if you had to move into a residential care home;
- ☐ the value of a house or land that you do not live in. This will be ignored for 26 weeks after you start:
  — to take reasonable steps to sell the property; *or*
  — to take legal action to occupy the property; *or*
  — to carry out essential repairs or alterations. The value may be disregarded for longer if you need more time to complete one of these things. It will be disregarded automatically for 26 weeks after you leave home due to divorce or estrangement. It may be disregarded for longer after you start any of the steps above.
  — business assets of a self-employed person, for as long as it takes to dispose of them;
  — arrears of attendance allowance, mobility allowance, or an income-related benefit for 52 weeks;
  — compensation for loss or damage to the home or possessions, eg, insurance payments;
  — money acquired for essential repairs or improvements to your home, for 6 months;*

— personal possessions, unless they were bought in order to claim more benefit;
— surrender value of an annuity or life insurance;
— capital in a trust fund which comes from a payment for personal injuries, eg, vaccine damage payments, compensation from an accident. The disregard will normally apply for 2 years for adults. There is no time limit for children.
— social fund payments;
— tax refund of mortgage interest relief.

* These time limits may be extended.

This is only a brief breakdown of what the rules say. If you are in any doubt about whether the DHSS will take account of any capital you have, or if they will treat you as having 'tariff income', get advice from one of the organisations in Appendix 10.

Mortgage arrears due to your partner's non-payment, when you are entitled to income support

If you have not been receiving your mortgage interest as part of your income support because your partner has defaulted on payments the DHSS believed s/he was making, you can ask the DHSS to pay the arrears of mortgage interest. The relevant provision says you can have the mortgage interest included as part of your housing costs even if you are not liable to pay it, where you have to pay the interest in order to keep your home and it is reasonable to pay you the money.

If you were entitled to income support for a period before you actually claimed it, you may be able to get a backpayment of benefit to cover that earlier period. You could use this to help clear your arrears.

You will be able to get benefit backdated in this way if, for the whole of the period before you claimed, you had 'good cause' for not doing so. Deciding whether you have 'good cause' involves looking at *why* you did not claim 'earlier' (see CPAG's *Rights Guide to Non-Means-Tested Social Security Benefits*, page 4, on meaning of 'good cause').

If you simply did not know whether or not you were entitled, and took no steps to find out, generally you will not be considered to have had 'good cause' for not claiming earlier. You are supposed to take 'reasonable steps' to find out what your rights are. Of course, if, for example, you have been too ill to find out and have been unable to get anyone else to enquire on your behalf, you might still be considered as having 'good cause'—it all depends on what you ought 'reasonably' to have done. If you *do* try to find out what your rights are, and are misinformed by someone who ought to know (eg, a solicitor, advice centre or the DHSS themselves), so that you are put off claiming, this may count as 'good cause' and allow benefit to be backdated when you claim later on.

If you would like more information about this rule, or would like to get help with persuading the DHSS that you had 'good cause' for not claiming before you did, contact one of the appropriate agencies listed in Appendix 10.

Specimen letters requesting a loan

The Manager
Westgate Building Society
High Street
Westgate

12 Park Road
Westgate

Account No: 246853

Dear Mr Brown,

Date:

I need to raise some money to do major repairs to my house. I will not be able to get a grant from the local authority so I will have to raise the money myself. A surveyor has told me which repairs are needed and I enclose a copy of his report. I have been able to get estimates of the cost of putting in the damp proof course and the rewiring. These two items will come to about £1,500, and the builder who came to see it thought that other work, costing a further £800, needed to be done. I will send you copies of the estimates as soon as I have them.

I would like to borrow £2,500 because that would then give me some extra in case any problems were discovered. It would also help me to buy the materials to redecorate (I would do that work myself).

My mortgage payments are £150 a month plus £4.50 for my mortgage protection policy. My rates are £35 a month and we spend about £25 a month on gas/electricity. That adds up to about £219.50.

I calculated that borrowing another £2,000 over the 20 years that my mortgage still has to run would cost another £26.60 a month which would take my costs up to £246.10 a month.

At the moment, I take home £600 a month, but we have just agreed our annual pay rise and I will be getting nearly £630 next month. My wife also gets £14.50 child benefit a week (£58 a month).

I have about £500 in the bank which I could use for the repairs, but I know there will be legal fees etc, and will need my savings for those.

Yours sincerely

JAMES GREEN

The Manager
Westgate Building Society
High Street
Westgate

23 Bank St
Westgate

Account No: 7532345

Dear Mr Brown,

Date:

I need to raise some money to do urgent repairs to my house. The roof is leaking and several of the window frames are badly rotted. I am enclosing copies of two estimates which you can see put the cost at about £3,000. I have applied to my local authority for a repairs grant. They have said I am probably eligible but they cannot let me know for a few weeks. If I receive a grant from them, I would only need to borrow £1,500.

I have spoken to my DHSS office, which is willing to meet increased payments on either amount and I enclose a letter from the manager confirming that.

As you know I work part-time and am meeting the capital payments out of the part of my income that the DHSS ignores. I have worked out that I would still be able to afford to do that if I borrowed more.

I am concerned about any fees that will be charged and would be grateful if you could give me an estimate of the costs involved in an additional mortgage.

Yours sincerely

MARY JONES

Legal Aid

If you have severe financial problems you may need a solicitor to advise you and, if necessary, to represent you in court, or arrange for a barrister to represent you in court. You will almost certainly need professional legal advice if you and your partner are separating.

HOW TO FIND A SOLICITOR

Your local citizens advice bureau or advice centre will be able to give you the names of solicitors who specialise in the areas of law on which you need advice, and who operate the Legal Aid Scheme.

HOW MUCH WILL IT COST?

Even if you qualify for legal aid because your disposable income (what is left after various deductions have been made) and your disposable capital are within the prescribed limits, you will normally still be required to make a contribution to your legal costs. (Note that the value of your home does *not* count as part of your disposable capital.) The rules for working out your contribution, if any, are quite complicated. There are two main kinds of non-criminal legal aid, the 'Green Form Scheme' and aid under a 'Legal Aid Certificate'. The rules for working out whether you qualify for help and, if so, what your contribution will be, are different for the two schemes; a Legal Aid Certificate is more generous. Another difference is that, with the Green Form Scheme, your solicitor works out immediately whether you are eligible, and any contribution is paid by you to your solicitor. With aid under a Legal Aid Certificate, the financial calculations are made by the DHSS, and any contribution by you is paid not to the solicitor but to the Law Society, which currently administers both types of legal aid. Under the Legal Aid Act 1988, the administration of these schemes will be transferred to a new Legal Aid Board. The Board, whose members are appointed by the Lord Chancellor, is expected to take over these duties in early 1989. We shall therefore now refer to the Legal Aid Board as the body responsible for granting legal aid.

THE GREEN FORM SCHEME

The official name for this is the 'Legal Advice and Assistance Scheme'. Under the scheme, those who come within the financial limits can obtain up to £50 worth of advice and assistance on practically any area of the law that is normally dealt with by a solicitor free of charge. This figure is increased to £90 in cases of undefended divorce or judicial separation.

The scheme allows your solicitor to write letters, negotiate on your behalf and obtain advice from a barrister about your case. However you cannot, apart from one or two exceptions, get help with the cost of legal proceedings, or representation at a court or Tribunal—although under the scheme your solicitor can give you advice on how to conduct your case in person.

Under the scheme, solicitors *can* do more than £50 (£90) of work if they obtain prior authority from the Law Society.

(Note that many solicitors also operate a fixed fee interview scheme, under which you can get up to half an hour's advice for £5, without regard to your means.)

The Government has indicated that it will require the Legal Aid Board to examine other methods of providing legal advice and assistance, including whether advice agencies could provide help of the kind which is currently provided by solicitors under the Green Form Scheme. This may mean that certain types of case (such as social security or housing problems) may in future be excluded from the Green Form Scheme altogether and that free advice on these kinds of problem will be available only from particular agencies or solicitors' firms who have been given special contracts for this purpose. For the present, however, Green Form assistance can be given on any matter of English law by any solicitor who operates the Legal Aid Scheme.

LEGAL AID UNDER A LEGAL AID CERTIFICATE

This is available for costs that will be incurred in connection with proceedings in a civil court. Your solicitor will help you to fill in the application form. It will normally take some weeks for the application to be processed, and it will not be possible to start court proceedings until the certificate is granted. However in urgent cases—for example, to obtain an injunction to exclude a violent spouse from the matrimonial home—an application for emergency legal aid can be made. In cases of extreme urgency, a solicitor can request an Emergency Certificate over the telephone.

To qualify for help, you have to pass two tests.

(i) You must come within the financial limits, as assessed by the DHSS. These change fairly frequently. You can check the current levels at your local citizens advice bureau, who will probably be able to give you a good idea as to whether you qualify and, roughly, what your contribution, if any, would be. You should note that, if you are married and living with your spouse, and not in dispute with him/her, your income and capital will be added together in working out whether you qualify for help.

(ii) You have to have reasonable grounds for taking or defending the action. This will be decided by the Legal Aid Board on the basis of the case put to them in the application form, and the supporting papers enclosed. They will not be pre-judging the matter—that is not their job—but rather coming to a decision as to whether it is reasonable for public funds to be spent in giving you financial assistance.

THE STATUTORY CHARGE

There is one particular feature of the Legal Aid Scheme which it is vital for anyone who seeks legal aid to understand. If you succeed in recovering or retaining money or property (including, for example, a house where there has been a dispute about who owns it), then you may, *in addition* to your assessed contribution, have to pay the legal costs incurred on your behalf that have not been covered by your contribution, out of that money or property. Normally, the costs of the winning party, or at any rate the bulk of the costs, are ordered to be paid by the losing party. However, if the losing party is *also* on legal aid, s/he will not in practice be ordered to pay your costs. This means that, in effect, you may well end up paying *all* your legal costs, even though you may initially have been assessed as having to make a nil contribution. Anyone on Legal Aid should therefore be aware of the 'statutory charge', as this feature of the scheme is called. Solicitors have a duty to explain how the charge operates to their legally-aided clients, and you should make sure that a full explanation is given to you.

Special rules apply where there have been matrimonial proceedings:

here the first £2,500 of a lump sum or property adjustment order is exempt from the charge.

Where it is property, rather than cash, that has been recovered or retained, the Legal Aid Board has discretion not to insist on immediate payment of the sum due to them, and also discretion to transfer the charge to different property. Where the property is a house, it is the practice to wait until the house is sold before recovering the money, or even, in some cases, to agree to transfer the charge (which has exactly the same status as, for example, a building society mortgage) to another house. This may be agreed if there is at least one dependent child who will be living with you in the second house, or if the reason for the move is to do with health, disability, or unemployment, and a refusal would cause hardship. Obviously, the equity in the second house must be sufficient to cover the amount owed to the Legal Aid Board.

There have been a number of very grim cases in recent years where an ex-spouse on Legal Aid who has been involved in a prolonged and expensive dispute over property with the former spouse has been left with very little of the sum awarded to her/him because of the way in which the statutory charge operates. It is always worth making every effort to negotiate a settlement prior to a court hearing rather than fighting the matter out in court. Though the court might award you a somewhat greater sum than has been offered to you to settle, you could still end up getting very much less, because of the extra costs you incurred in taking the matter to court—costs that may have to be paid out of the sum awarded to you.

Useful addresses

If you would like further advice on any of the subjects covered in this guide, the following local organisations may be able to help.

- ☐ A law centre.
- ☐ A citizens advice bureau.
- ☐ A neighbourhood advice centre.
- ☐ A housing aid centre.
- ☐ A local authority welfare rights officer.

You can find out the addresses of these agencies and people from the telephone directory, local authority offices or libraries.

If you are unable to find help in your area, one of the following groups may be able to advise you, or refer you to someone who can.

SHAC (The London Housing Aid Centre)
189a Old Brompton Road
London SW5 0AR
Tel: 01-373 7276

(Specialises in advice on all problems to do with housing.)

National Council for One Parent Families
255 Kentish Town Road
London NW5 2LX
Tel: 01-267 1361

(Advice to one parent families and single pregnant women on all areas, including housing, social security and divorce.)

National Association of Citizens Advice Bureaux
Myddleton House
115/123 Pentonville Road
London N1 9LZ
Tel: 01-833 2181

Gingerbread
35 Wellington Street
London WC2E 7BN
Tel: 01-240 0953

(A national organisation for single parents, with local branches. Offers general advice and can refer on to specialist agencies.)

Women's Aid Federation (England)
374 Featherstone Street
London EC1
Tel: 01-837 9316

Welsh Women's Aid
38-48 Crwys Road
Cardiff CF2 4NN
Tel: 0222 390 874 (9.30am-3.00pm)

(Refers battered women (with or without children) to refuges. Gives advice on injunctions, divorce, housing, social security. Referrals to sympathetic solicitors or local women's aid groups.)

Other organisations mentioned in this Guide:

Building Societies' Association
3 Savile Row
London W1X 1AF
Tel: 01-437 0655

Child Benefit Centre
PO Box 1
Newcastle Upon Tyne
NE88 1AA
Tel: 091-416 6722

DHSS
Family Credit Unit
Government Buildings
Warbreck Hill
Blackpool FY2 0YF
Tel: 0253-500050

District Land Registry Office
HM Land Registry
32 Lincoln's Inn Fields
London WC2A 3PH
Tel: 01-405 3488

Land Charges Registry
Burrington Way
Plymouth PL5 3LP
Tel: 0752 779831

Law Society
113 Chancery Lane
London WC2A 1PL
Tel: 01-242 1222

Useful publications

WELFARE BENEFITS

National Welfare Benefits Handbook (1988/89 edition), price £5.50 (£2.50 for claimants) p&p incl, and *Rights Guide to Non-Means-Tested Social Security Benefits* (1988/89 edition), price £4.50 (£2 for claimants) p&p incl. Both books are available from CPAG Ltd, 1-5 Bath Street, London EC1V 9PY.

HOUSING

SHAC publishes a wide range of detailed housing rights guides. A full list of publications is available from the Publications Officer, SHAC (The London Housing Aid Centre), 189a Old Brompton Road, London SW5 0AR.

PUBLICATIONS FROM OTHER ORGANISATIONS

Shared Ownership, available from the Housing Corporation, 149 Tottenham Court Road, London W1, free.

All about loft and tank insultation and *Home Improvement Grants*. Both available from the Department of the Environment, Building 3, Victoria Road, South Ruislip, Middx. HA4 0NZ, both free.

Defending Possession Proceedings, available from Legal Action Group, 242 Pentonville Road, London N1 9UN. Part IV of this book specifically deals with mortgage possession actions.

Index